Eyota Voices

Stories and Poems

D. E. Brobst

Table of Contents

Special thanks to my wife, children and extended family for their trust and inspiration. Thanks to all former students from Winthrop High School to Apollo High School who inspired me with their creativity. Thanks to the Eyota voices.

About the Author

Eyota was a small town where characters in this book were growing up. In my present life, Eyota stories and characters chase me in my dreams. My Id, Ego, Superego, and resulting sublimation, projection, narcissism, and the all-too-frequent tintinnabulation of bells are the fabric of my being.

Superior! That's what Oscar Matteson told Leon Eyota means. When I think of superior, it's not Eyota that comes to mind. It's Lake Superior. The only water I remember while growing up in Eyota was the trickle of the creek as it struggled to avoid disappearing into the earth a block south of the railway depot. There was enough water in the little creek that snaked its way east toward Dover that the railroad built five bridges between Eyota and Dover. No one ever referred to it as Bear Creek. Years after I and the characters in this book moved away, a dam was built at Bear creek headwaters that formed Chester Woods Park.

Author's Note

Saturday Night

Eyota July 1959

Free movie shows
interrupted by
Rumbling freights
On silver rails
Saturday night outdoors.

9:45 p.m.

Blinds close at midnight
Lovers cruise
Two blocks of Front
and Center Streets.
Saturday nights outdoors.

I learned hypocrisy early
Watching Sunday grape juice drinkers
Protestants drinkers double-park

At the Municipal
Saturday nights.

A block away,

Catholic confessors

Emerge smiling.

Pious. Cleansed.

After Saturday Mass.

The pious gather

After headaches and Anacin

For Church and Mass

Sunday mornings indoors.

Leon *Intro*

Maybe it is time for me to tell you a few Eyota stories. The narrator and a variety of Eyota characters, like my brother and a few of his friends, will also tell you stories. Bev, one of the narrator's high school classmates, was relentless in asking him when he was going to complete a second book after having published Knock Until the Dog Barks in 2013. The narrator decided to allow characters to tell their own Eyota stories.

If you, the reader, recognize yourself in any of the characters' stories, they will offer no apology. They only exist between these covers. If you recognize yourself in some stories, the narrator may or may not have intended for that to happen.

Thank you, Bev, for encouraging the author to invent me.

Leon

I always disliked being Leon. I mean, no one, not even my best friends, called me Lee. Somehow, I was always and forever Leon. Leon: two syllables instead of one. It always made me feel old. Witty is my brother. Somehow two syllables fit him just fine. He's two years older than me, but he's ten years smarter and much more mature.

It is still warm in Eyota when I begin writing my story. There is a full moon and I am home alone. Shadows stretch long and lean from tree trunks in the backyard where we pitch our tents, so we can escape the southern Minnesota tropical days and get a little relief from a humid breeze at night.

Eyota is a drowsy town that always seems to be yawning. It didn't have or need a local newspaper. Local gossip spreads before five o'clock and is embellished during supper. Rochester folks had dinner. We called it supper. We had dinner. They had lunch. Witty said calling dinner supper was hayseedish. The day's most interesting events usually happened around 5:00 in the afternoon. That was when the mail was stuffed in the post office mailboxes. There was no home delivery in Eyota. The post office was located directly across the street from Selmy's Shop and Save, where the 5:00 p.m. post office rush began. Those who didn't stop at Selmy's for a few necessities gathered in twos and threes outside the post office. The lobby was too small for more to linger. Some of the men took their mail to Charlie's pool hall, where they opened it while slurping beer. Charlie listened to the chatter at the bar and offered his opinion on whatever the topic might be.

Not much exciting had happened since a few of the spring graduates had enlisted in the army and a pregnant girl had dropped out of school three months before graduation. All of this nearly resulted in a morality campaign, but it had been forgotten in a short time as townspeople became more interested in planting vegetable and flower gardens, mowing the lawn and waiting for the rhubarb to ripen. The price of sugar, flour, coffee, bread and milk hadn't gone up a penny or two like last fall, so there everything seemed to calm in Eyota.

Earth's Chains

We sit together apart,
A trinity no sermon can explain,
Chains of twisted dandelion stems,
Each head a tuft of yellow, some grey,
a splash of sun.

We are Earth and she is ours,
But only for the moment
'til a cloud
passes.

When my shape returns,
Another piece of life creeps
to suspend me
between Earth and Sky.

Me and Witty

Favorite Song Me: Bird Dog

Witty: Rebel Rouser

They named my brother William Amos Holman. Everyone called him Witty. They named me Leon Arnold. Everyone called me Leon. Witty was two years older than me. I worshipped him. He tolerated me.

"Come on, little brother. Down just a block below Matteson's house, where the creek flows under the second bridge. Down there. We can build our hideaway." He clasped both hands on my face. He was fifteen. My hero. My god. He was Greek, with his black curly hair twisting 'round his forehead. He even smelled good. And he wore his clothes good, no matter what he chose, from his Sunday blue suit to his everyday blue jeans and striped t-shirts. At one time in our lives, I swore I would follow him anywhere, even to the church where our Methodist temperance movement mother and President of the Women's Society of Christian Service insisted we attend and pretend to be holy.

At Sunday services, Mother poked me awake just as the Witty scooped a handful of communion-leavened white-bread cubes into his mouth. I hadn't yet been confirmed, so I passed the plate to Mom. I didn't have a suit like Witty. His was what I think they call tweed. I wore the same cotton pullover every Sunday, even in the summer. When the twenty-minute pastoral prayer began, I dozed off and on to the drone of his voice. Mother kept poking me. How did she know when to do that? She should have had her eyes closed in prayer. Witty sat with folded hands like the angel he wasn't. Mother sat between us. Dad? He went fishing with Earl Selmy on Sundays, the only day the Shop and Save was closed.

Witty nudged Mother. She spits on her handkerchief, embroidered gift of aunt Neddie, a temperance queen if there was such a thing, and wipes the slobber from my sleepy lips.

Aunt Neddie sat us down most Saturday nights at the kitchen table to share cartoon booklets instructing us in the evils of drink. I had hidden under my mattress cover the crudely drawn black and white pornographic cartoon booklet my friend Freddy had given me. I peeled back the cover and fumbled to find the book. I had run my fingers over the drawings so many times that some private parts were smudged. I shined a flashlight beneath the quilt aunt Neddie had stitched for me. The quilt had flaming candles, crosses wreathed in pink and blue flowers and the words, "Now I lay me down to sleep. I pray the Lord my soul to keep." I didn't know who would keep my soul if I died with the booklet under my mattress cover.

Eyota was a small town with small houses and businesses located without a lake nearby in southeastern Minnesota. It took about fifteen minutes to drive highway 14 to the Rochester Mayo Clinic. I interviewed Oscar Matteson for a school article. I won first prize at the *Eyota Echoes* writing contest when I was in seventh grade. Witty was in ninth grade. He won second prize for his *Eyota Echoes article* on the basketball team's loss to Rochester in the Region Basketball Tourney. Witty was on the "B" team. I was his team's manager. To be honest, I was actually the go-fer. Go-fer the athletic tape. Go-fer more basketballs. Go-fer more dry towels. Go-fer the water jugs. Go-fer my jersey. At least they didn't instruct me to go-fer their jock straps.

I was awarded $2.50 for my English paper. Before I wrote it, I walked across the gravel road separating our little house from Oscar Matteson's big house. I believe he inherited it from Milo Matteson, one of the town founders, but I'm not sure. His house was a mansion in my seventh-grade imagining. Our house on the eastern edge of Eyota was located only three blocks from Front Street, where Selmy's Shop and Save was located. Oscar Matteson's house rose from the green lawn of an entire half-block, the last block beyond ours. I often cursed, silently, of course, while pushing the me-powered lawn mower while I watched a caretaker follow a self-propelled gas-powered mower over the emerald expanse of Oscar's lawn. I thought dandelions were quite pretty when they bloomed in our yard and Mom liked them. I often sat among dandelions as ants crawled over my legs and arms while I made elaborate necklaces and what I imagined to be Roman crowns from dandelion stems circled and ringed together to place on my royal head. Oscar's lawn grew nothing but green.

Eyota is Superior

It was a short walk from my house to Oscar Matteson's. I was afraid to knock. He was old. He was older than Aunt Neddie. Older than anyone I had ever seen or known. I knocked. Waited. Knocked again.

"Yes," he said. "Hello, Leon. Your mother said you were coming to talk to me about Eyota for a school report you are writing."

"Come in. Sit," he limped.

I sat down on the arm of a rosy pink peony fabric that I was afraid would suffocate me if I sank into it.

Oscar began by talking about his grandfather, Milo Matteson, who owned the farmland that is now Eyota. He is lucky. I mean, Oscar, Oscar said he was lucky to own the biggest piece of Eyota. He laughed. I asked him what Eyota meant. He said it means superior. He said it is an Indian word. He laughed and said Eyota was once much bigger than Rochester.

I asked him how could that be true? He said it was because of the railroad. Eyota was the place where passengers and freight could transfer. Transfer? I wasn't sure what transfer meant. I think he knew that I didn't understand.

He said Eyota was the place where the railroad came to a why. I asked him why?

"It's spelled W Y E. One direction led to Plainview and one direction led to Chatfield. The line stopped at Eyota. Now you know why," he chuckled.

I wanted to ask him why the wye stopped in Eyota and didn't go on to Rochester, but Oscar seemed eager to tell me more.

"Eyota streets were laid out on the farmland owned by my grandfather, Milo Matteson, by investor Samuel E. Everett, a speculator from New York State. A downtown district, built only on the south side of the street, faced the railroad yard. Mr. Everett built a hotel called the Everett House. It was located along the street facing the depot. I don't know what happened to it. It was gone by the time I was born. Maybe it burned down. There's a project for you. Maybe you can find out."

Oscar coughed. Stood up and limped to the door.

"Leon," he said. "Tell your teacher that is what I remember at this moment of our Eyota." He stood ready to close the door. "Um… one more thing. Would you stop by the drugstore and buy me a couple of cigars?"

That is the end of my report. I hope you like it.

Witty wasn't happy that I had received so much attention for my report. After all, I am the younger brother. I am shy. Witty is not. Everybody likes Witty. Our two-year age difference in addition to my being about six inches shorter was obvious to everyone in Eyota. I shouldn't complain because I have Freddy. Witty was always opening new doors for himself and slamming them in my face.

Reparation

When I was nine goin' on ten
I couldn't find a nickel
To buy myself a smile
So I rubbed my copper cent piece
'gainst my cotton pocket lining
until it shined like momma's kettles.

Right after that first July week
Someone plastered a Penny Arcade poster
On the lumberyard fence.
I rubbed my copper cent piece
And dreamed the sun
Reflected my future.

A fortune-telling Gypsy Witch in a red and gold cage
Drew me to slide my shiny gold cent piece
Into the cold black slot.
She cranked her head, spun her eyes
Rattled her wrist toward mine.
Rapping my youth with her knuckled grin

She birthed a card that read:
For a penny, you would sell your soul.

Weeks later, a sunfish spun at hook's end
Splashed its lifeless shadow across my face.
Past the lumberyard fence
Where the Gypsy Witch poster
Drooped like the skin from grandma's arms
I ran home for paste
To repair the end of summer.

Leon

Aunt Neddie

Aunt Neddie believed that the Methodist Church would save Witty's and my souls. Whenever she came for her two-week visit, the first thing she did was to remove everything from the cupboards. She scrubbed them clean. I think she was also trying to scrub our little minds. "Little man," she said as she patted the chair seat next to her at the kitchen table. I think I was eight or nine then. I hated being called "little man." Mother had disappeared somewhere into the sanctity of the forbidden storage room. I often sneaked in there to admire the shotgun no one was ever supposed to touch.

"Here. Sit down beside me, Lee." She ruffled my hair and smiled. "I have some readings here for you that your father has not heeded." She patted my head as if that would help me understand. "Look at this skinny man. Here," she pointed her finger to the black and white cartoon drawing. "See that bottle lying next to him in the gutter?"

I nodded. *How could I miss it?*

"That bottle contains the devil's liquid. It is cursed. It destroys those who drink it. Do you understand?"

I thought I understood, but I really didn't. I looked up into her wire-rimmed blue eyes. Oh God, how I wanted to please her. She was frailer than Mother and not nearly as smiley, but there was a gleam in her eye that could easily be mistaken for a twinkle. "Yes, auntie. Dad drinks beer."

"Oh, my little sweetheart, that. That I don't approve of, your dad's mostly a nice man, and he mostly treats your mother decently, but the evil of," she stopped. Caught her breath with her hand pushed gently against her sternum. "Evil of drink," she gasped. Inhaled slowly, plucked the lacey handkerchief from her bosom, nodded her head and sniffled.

I moved closer to her and leaned my head on her arm. I didn't know what was wrong with her.

"Look at this," she continued when she recovered. "Do you know where that man in the picture is lying?"

"Yes, Auntie. It looks like the gutter outside of Charlie's Tavern."

"And look at this one. My smart little man. What does it say?"

I had no idea what the caption meant, but her warmth comforted me. "It says: Al-co-hold is one of," I stammered. "One of the greatest causes of mind disease."

"Wonderful. Yes. You are so smart, my little sweetheart. Let's read this little poem created by Mary Scott Russell, former president of the Georgia Women's Christian Temperance Union: 'Mary Had a Little Lamb.'"

Mary and her little lamb live on a great big farm.

Mary loves her little lamb and keeps it safe from harm.

It follows her to school, but it waits out on the grass.

There really isn't *anything* a lamb could do in class!

But Mary studies earnestly each day she is in school.

Good citizens must be informed! She knows that that's the rule.

She's learning what to eat and drink to keep her well and *fit*.

She learns, too, what she *must not* drink—and alcohol is *it."*

From The Atlantic May 27, 218

She squeezed me so tightly that I felt my head press against her breasts. *Boobs,* I thought. *Aunt Neddie has boobs?* Maybe she felt I had fallen too close even for her not to notice. She eased me gently into my chair and whispered, "Would you like some rhubarb pie?" I felt vibrations when she put her arms around me and squeezed the breath out of me.

Mother slipped into the room from nowhere. "You will. I know you will always listen to Aunt Neddie and me. You see how evil devil drink can be," Mother said. She handed me a chocolate chip cookie after I finished the rhubarb pie.

Leon

I helped Witty set up our pup tent in our backyard. He was in ninth grade and I was in seventh. I didn't know how big our age difference had become until Mr. Thorman, the evilest physical education teacher ever, forced seventh graders, us and the ninth graders to join the sophomores for football blocking drills. I didn't belong on the same turf with Witty and his buddies J.D. and Jeb Wicker, much less in the same locker room with them.

So there we stood naked. I didn't want to raise my eyes from my feet when I pulled down my jockey underwear. I didn't know where to look. I allowed my eyes to rest on Witty. He slipped out of his underwear and backslapped his latest best friends the Witty Twins. I gasped and hung my head in shame. I had been praying for just one chest hair. Witty told me about J.D. and Jeb's cool new microscope kit their parents had given them for their birthday. "Don't tell Mom and Dad," Witty confided in me. "You can see the most amazing things under a microscope." Witty told me about the pubic hair he and the twins had examined under the microscope.

Sometimes Witty was just plain mean to me and Freddy. I can't explain why we continued to ride bicycles with him the two miles east of town to the dump and haunted house. He always insisted on being the commander of whatever we three did together and that scared me.

It was not an easy ride for me and Freddy. The road had ruts in it and I'm sure they were caused by the iron-wheeled manure spreader Max Freemont towed to his fields when the road was soft after rain. When it was dry, we had to swerve around cow manure that had fallen on the road. I turned too sharp to avoid a stinking clump. I hit loose gravel and slid from the road to the ditch.

Witty was a quarter mile ahead of me and Freddy. Freddy was ahead of me and didn't look back. I lay there for a while, feeling my arms to see if I could move them. My elbows and knees were burning and oozing blood. I wanted to cry. I didn't want to look ahead or go back.

I tipped my bike upright. Rolled down my shirtsleeve to cover the road rash. Hopped on and pedaled as fast as I could without hitting any more chunks of cow shit. Some of it was mixed with straw. I slammed the coaster brake. The odor of manure clung to the air. My jeans were clean. My shirtsleeves were dusty but were free of manure. "Shit," I said out loud. I wasn't far from the dump. My nose directed me to my bike's front tire. There was a pancake-flat wad of shirt stuck to the tire and the rim.

"Hey, come on, slowpoke," Freddy waved and hollered. He and Witty sat drinking Dr. Peppers under the dump sign, NO TRESPASSING. Witty had his .22 rifle beside him. I pedaled up to them and sat down. Old reliable Freddy offered me a Dr. Pepper and handed Witty a pack of Kools.

“You gotta get your ass in shape, little brother.” Witty blew smoke rings and coughed like a real smoker. I don’t think he inhaled.

“Yeah,” I turned my eyes to the ground. Witty always said things to me that made me do that. “Dad knows you took the gun?”

“No, you little shit. And you better not rat on me. I’m here to kill rats!” He took a long drag and blew smoke into the blue, cloudless sky.

Witty swung the .22 in a wide arc over my head and lowered it in super slow motion close to the top of my head. The sneer on his face and the blank look in his eyes made me swear I was looking at the devil. I froze at my place. Witty slowly lowered the gun. I felt the barrel resting on my shoulder.

“Witty! Stop! This isn’t funny,” Freddy yelled. He tripped over his bike kickstand and knocked his bike over.

I was so terrified that I didn’t hear a sound. Blood pounded in my ears. *Loaded? Was the rifle loaded?*

Witty pointed the rifle to the sky. Lowered it again and shot a hole in the O on the No Trespassing sign. “Good shot, huh?” he coughed and spat on the ground. “Go get some cans and set ’em up on top of the refrigerator over there.”

“The rats,” Freddy shuddered. I think he was more afraid of the rats than I was of Witty or the rifle. Just last week, he had told me that his dad sent him to sack potatoes in the small warehouse attached to the store. The light switch was about three feet inside on the wall to the right of the entry. Ever since he had been a kid, Freddy hated fumbling for the switch. Just as he reached for the switch, he felt something brush his pant leg as it scurried over his shoe. He shrieked and flipped on the light. Beatrice meowed as she sat atop a fifty-pound gunnysack of potatoes.

"Don't be girly," Witty taunted. "See that hole in the sign. The commander hits the bull's eye every time. Don't forget that!"

No One Shoots Songbirds

No one shoots songbirds anymore
Not even Chief Red Cloud
Who bangs his wagon against
My car's virgin fender.
It's strange to watch robins
Pull at the earth while a child's
War whoops splinter my window screen.

I played once, pretending grandpa's farm,
It was African Jungle. Striped barn cats
Were my tiger prey.

I played once until I grew into hunting boots
With rawhide laces and silver eyelets.
Oh, how I grew. Out of myself into manhood
Straight out of Outdoor Life and Sear's Catalog.

I learned to use my peep sights
To keep my observations silent.
I learned to stalk grouse
To still shiver in my spine.
I learned to cradle my 12-gauge shotgun

To protect its barrel from bramble scratches.

But now I walk alone

With silence

Disturbing

My hunt.

Freddy Selmy

Author

Freddy Selmy punched the wounded cash register key, once again catching his fingernail on the torn plastic key cover. The eighty-cent key was one of nine in need of repair, but Freddy's father, Earl, having pondered the wisdom of high-financial advice gleaned from the newly published *Changing Times – The Kiplinger Magazine*, had decided that the advantage of a depreciation allowance on a new cash register was slight in comparison to the disadvantage of the initial cash outlay for a new machine. Freddy cursed, repented, flipped his forefinger under the metal tongue holding the one-dollar bills, inserted the bill on the soggy pile and scraped two slick dimes from among the grit of the change compartment.

"Thank you, Mrs. Bellamy." Freddy smiled as he handed her two dimes. He felt guilty for letting his eyes wander over the hairy mole on her chin, but the mothball odor of her clothes reassured him that his youthful perception was correct. She was a browning remnant of a faded era he cared to know nothing about.

The screened door rattled shut, its metal bottom rasping against the cement as she exited. Lights blinked as frozen food compressors surged. The red second hand rotated smoothly across the face of the new Hires Root Beer clock. 1:57, three hours, thirty-three minutes until closing. He fingered the soiled list his father had taped to the cash register. “Pay bread and milkmen cash. Write it down. Rinse bulk wieners. After closing, turn off the meat case lights. Spread sweeping compound. Sort and fill three five-pound and two ten-pound bags of red potatoes. Throw away rotten ones. Remove fly stickers above the produce. Hang new ones. Throw away last week’s special signs.”

Every Tuesday, the list was the same except for additional stains on the paper. Freddy of thought of himself as the family martyr, but he never dwelled on it. Fourteen was not a magic age for Freddy. The everyday drudgery of the grocery store, his routine chatter with frequent customers drained humor and creativity from his mind and will. Freddy’s mother and father launched their little boat at Reed’s Landing on the Mississippi and fished from dawn to dusk every summer Tuesday—abandoning Freddy to be Eyota’s youngest businessman. The summer afternoon droned on. Few customers wandered in, Freddy pulled the 24-to-a-carton Kotex trash box from beneath the sales counter, peered through the glass display window facing the street, crouched beneath the counter and lit a cigarette.

Smoke curled in wide ribbons with thick blue edges. Freddy felt a surge of forbidden pleasure. *This was escape!* He vowed that he would no longer dream of delivering groceries and being propositioned by home-alone housewives as thanks for his courteous delivery if God would keep his smoking and his delivery fantasies secret. His face grew hot from the shame of bargaining. He crushed the cigarette under his heel, wrapped the butt in tissue and dropped it into the Kotex box.

He hastily shoved the box under the counter as he heard the rasp of the screened door. He hoped the heat had left his cheeks. Stooping to pick up scrap paper, Freddy rose behind the sales counter to meet old Sam Gorman's sweaty gaze.

I wish he had died last night, Freddy grimaced. *Why can't he just die and leave me alone? Every day he shuffles through the door for his can of snuff. Every day his face reminds me of my joking about sex. One of these nights, he will die. It has to come very soon. He is so old. He'll die and take my sinful request to his grave. He's a foolish, dirty old man. No one will believe what he says if he talks. He's old. Has lived too long. It's time for him to die. Die, Sam. Take our secret with you.*

Sam's snorting cough, his gurgling, his spitting into his crusty, red handkerchief made Freddy retch.

"How's my boy today? Folks gone fishin' again?" Sam mumbled beneath the handkerchief clutched in his hand.

Freddy glared. Nodded. Shoved the snuff across the counter. "Twenty-five cents," he said. "My god," he gulped. Spasms of heat rushed from his neck to his cheeks as his eyes snagged on the little packet next to the quarter. He couldn't look up, he wanted to hide and wanted to lash out at Sam. *Bury him!* He felt his hand being drawn toward the glistening no-bigger-than-a-half-dollar shining packet.

Selmy's Shop and Save Market continued to fester in the July heat. The only sound surrounding Freddy and Sam was the drone of refrigeration compressors. Freddy's eyes darted bird-quick from the packet to meet Sam's sweating face.

"I got'em, yah," Sam nodded. "At the drugstore. Like we talked, I would."

No, you crazy fool, Freddy thought. *It was all a stupid joke.*

"You keep this one now," Sam said. "You keep it. I can get you more." He pushed the packet close to Freddy.

"I… I… I don't need it," Freddy whispered as he hid his eyes on the floor. The screened door scraped shut.

Freddy brushed the prophylactic packet from the counter and slipped it into his jeans pocket. *What would he do with it?* He knew Witty Holman carried one in his wallet. He liked to show Freddy and the other kids the circular indentation in the leather. *He couldn't do that. Suppose Mother found his wallet?* Sam and he shared this secret, but worse, he had told Sam about his desire for and fear of sex. He should throw the rubber in the bulk Kotex box beneath the counter, but it might spill out somehow if Dad emptied its trash. Sam would come back every day at the same time, and either his mother or father might be working. *What if Sam told?*

Freddy feared word would be spread through Eyota. He imagined every customer knowing about his sinful desires. There was no escape. He was into it now and there was no going back. Sam would die. If not soon, and if Sam keeps silent through the summer, Freddy will be back in school. He wouldn't have to look Sam in the face and remember, but that didn't solve this day's encounter, or tomorrow's, or the rest of the weeks' encounters with Sam. Freddy feared meeting Sam Gorman's eyes.

2:15 p.m. is a sleepy time in Eyota. Freddy slid the trash box from beneath the counter, sat on his haunches and lit a cigarette. He closed his eyes tightly after watching the circular spasm of white smoke float like breasts. He fondled them. Shoulders and arms floated beyond the breasts, but there was never a face. He caressed the packet burning in his jeans pocket. The phone rang, Freddy sensed that it was Mother calling. *Had she been watching?* He fumbled for the packet in his pocket, one hand in his pocket, the other reaching for the phone. The phone rang again and again. Freeing hand and packet, he grabbed a handkerchief from his back pocket, wrapped the packet, and shoved both in his front pocket as he answered the call.

Freddy quickly recovered his practiced businessman's composure. He scribbled items on a notepad: a quart of milk, six eggs, sardines, and two bananas. He wasted the remainder of the afternoon in conversations about the 95-degree heat and high humidity. 5:30 p.m. arrived. He sacked the delivery order, loaded it in his bicycle basket, slipped a pack of Kools into his jeans pocket and pedaled off toward the Bellamy house. After supper, Witty Holman would expect Freddy to deliver cigarettes that Witty would distribute to his friends, making him king of the hill in his little circle of Eyota buddies. While riding his bike the few blocks to the Bellamy house, Freddy imagined wading in the creek beyond the second railway bridge. He lowered the kickstand on his girly bike. This is Betty Bellamy's door he was about to knock on. He knew everyone in town called her Bouncing Betty. It was a week ago at the second bridge that Witty Holman had told him, the Witty twins and Leon Holman, that the reason people called her “Bouncing Betty” was because Betty liked to wear low-cut blouses.

Sweat dripped from Freddy’s brow and grew like bruises on the brown grocery bag. He knocked as a voice came from the darkened interior, “Come on in! Sure is hot out there,” Betty bounced to the door, opened it and motioned to the dining room table.

“Yah,” Freddy said, tasting salty sweat from his lips.

“Coke to cool you?” she asked as she disappeared into another room.

He stuttered, “Uh uh… ah… sure… but… but I have to collect $2.29 for the groceries.”

“Sit,” she said from the next room. “I’m getting the money and the Coke.

Freddy sat and wished to God she would hurry. The gang would be at the swimming hole in half an hour. He needed to be there to deliver the beer and cigs.

Betty stood before him with a perspiring glass of Coke. He nodded his thanks, grabbed the glass with both hands and felt it squirt, crash and spill on the table’s brilliant white cloth. He looked up to see the brown drizzle of Coke snake from Mrs. Manley’s neck to her cleavage.

"Oooh," she moaned and laughed. "That does feel good," she laughed again with her head tossed back.

Freddy jerked his handkerchief from his jeans pocket. Offered it to her at the same time, the rubber packet seemed to float from the handkerchief to splash with an overwhelming silent slap as it landed and stuck to the tablecloth. Freddy's libido died. *It is good,* a distant voice whispered, *to go quietly now, to slip away on the wings of warm where all the light is pure.* A warm arm rested on his shoulder and tugged gently. Freddy felt he was being transported across the carpet, across an abyss, when she smiled and curled her hand around the packet. He raised his eyes to hers; the same sweaty gaze as Sam Gorman's met his.

"My god," Freddy whispered.

Mrs. Manley's Bikini

A droplet of sun quivers

on the stem

of her daisy petal

navel.

In the shadow

of her hip swing

pollen showers

supple seedlings.

Come fall

her eyes

having crystallized

the risen sap

will unzip

sugar-seeking lips.

In the Near Hot Grass

I shovel the school lawn's spring litter
Into my battered eyes.

A sophomore girl's hair is a khaki tent
Staked to her ears with pearl studs.
She gathers he knees in front,
Erects a moat no one must cross.
Against her sky, three trees
Leafless, sapless
Stripe her carnival body
With gently-brushed shadows.

Who has painted her face?
Was it the muscle-shirted bodies
Sizzling in the near-hot grass?
Or was it the fuzzy-bottomed clouds
Copulating in the barebacked blue?

Brushing aside a flap of hair
I try to fold my thirty years together.
My basement carpet has sucked in spring juices.
My groin has fallen asleep.

I can’t imagine pulling up stakes

Or unhooking a pearl from a clown’s pierced ear.

Leon

- **Witty**

The pup tent! I didn't know then why it was called a pup tent. I never looked it up. Mom and Dad gave me permission to sleep in the pup tent nearly every night the summer before I entered eighth grade. Witty was supposed to check on me while he slept on the screened porch. I remember overhearing Mom saying to Dad after supper, "Witty is so grown up. He'd never let anything happen to little Leon." They didn't know the Witty I knew.

Witty helped me pound the railroad spikes through the tent loops to secure it to the ground. We positioned it just a few feet from where the lean-to, makeshift garage shelter our father had tried to erect **it**. I think he worked mostly on it after he came home from Charlie's Pool Hall on summer evenings. His biggest mistake was chaining Buster, our German Shepherd, to one of the supporting posts. One afternoon Buster smelled heat. He took off in hot pursuit of Reverend Paddock's bitch and tore down the whole damned lean-to. Dad threatened to donate the dog to the Mayo Clinic to be used for research. The dog was Dad's best friend. He never followed through. Buster was his fishing pal.

The night we planned to harass the Wicker twins, we asked Freddy Selmy to sleep over with us. We knew he had a key to his dad and mom's grocery store, so we could celebrate there, drink pop, talk smart and smoke cigs after our having a little fun. Freddy arrived a few minutes after we drove in the last spike. He had his sleeping bag strapped onto his back. He got off his bike and lifted a grocery bag from the bike basket his dad had attached, so Freddy could deliver small items to customers.

"Hey, Freddy. Whatcha got in the bag?"

Freddy fumbled around in the back for what seemed like five minutes. He pulled out a package of Oreos. Opened it and handed the package to me. Freddy was a real pal. Witty stuffed three Oreos into his mouth chewed and mumbled, "You know Wickers have lights in their tent. And a radio."

"Wow!" Freddy said.

"And," Witty continued. "Their dad put twin bed mattresses in the tent for them." We gotta have some fun with them tonight. I've got a plan."

Witty took two more Oreos and crammed them into his mouth, chewed and chewed until I was ready to burst for wanting to hear about his plan. Freddy took a cookie and handed the package to me.

"I brought Coca-Cola too," Freddy said. "And an opener."

Witty reached across the army blanket we had spread to pad the hard ground. He slapped Freddy on the back. "Maybe we can be blood brothers after tonight."

"The plan. The plan, Witty?" I knew he was a tease, but this was irritating me. He liked to keep me in suspense to make me feel inferior. At least, that's what I thought.

Witty swallowed as he uncapped the Coke. "You know," he said, looking at Freddy and ignoring me. "We should have brought some aspirin mixed with Coke, I've heard, gives you a buzz."

"Nah," Freddy said. "I tried that last Tuesday at the store. Nothing happened." I still got just as angry when Sam Gorman winked and asked me to wrap two of the biggest skin-on wieners for him."

They didn't offer me a Coke, so I just took one from the six-pack, opened it and looked at Witty. "The plan, Witty. What's the plan?"

He crossed his legs Indian style and began. "First, we get a bucket for each of us. I'll put you in charge of that, Leon."

"Witty," I said as politely as I could. "Please call me Lee." He looked at me like he had swallowed a worm.

He continued, "I and Freddy will go to Freddy's store and get some paper bags, some matches, and apples. You have some, right?"

"Yah," Freddy said. "But I just filled ten and five-pound paper bags yesterday from the 100-pound bag of potatoes. There were more rotten potatoes than usual. I forgot to bury them in Mom's garden."

Witty Jack-in-the-box jumped and made a bulge in the tent top. "Brilliant!"

I looked at Freddy. He looked back at me. "What?" we said at the same time.

“This is so damned brilliant and easy, Freddy. Don’t you see? We don’t need to swipe apples from your store. We’ll use rotten potatoes. Brilliant!”

Freddy grabbed Witty’s arm and pulled him to his knees. “Weapons. Right. Rotten potato weapons will burst like grenades. We need ’em to stink up the Wickers. Wow. ”

“We need a way to get them out of their tent, see?” Witty said. He kneeled and spread his hands over the air as if he were blessing us.

“Listen, I have an idea, Freddy. Your dog poops on your lawn, right?”

“That’s gross. Of course.”

“And do you pick it up?

“Dammit, Witty. That’s way too nasty and way too personal. Do I ever ask you for an I.D. when you want a pack of cigs from the store?”

“Freddy, Listen… listen, we are not talking about cigarettes here. We are talking… listen carefully… we are talking about turds… dog turds… squishy ones”

Freddy shuddered in fear of Witty’s wisdom as well as being banished from his presence. “Huh?”

“Let me lay out this simple plan. Before we attack the Wickers with rotten potatoes, we put Freddy’s dog’s turds in a paper bag., remember? They gotta be squishy fresh, Freddy.”

I sat there like I wasn't there. Nobody looked at me. Nobody cared whether I had an opinion or not. I loved the mystery, but I hated what they might want me to do.

"Squishy fresh?" Freddy said.

"Not like your dad's days-old bakery goods," Witty laughed and pointed his finger at Freddy. "Fresh."

"You gonna come and pick up the fresh poop?" Freddy asked.

"Why not? I'd clean it off a baby's butt if you agree to light the bag of shit on fire outside the Wicker's tent and run like hell." Witty was so excited he started drooling. Wiped the slime on his sleeve and said, "And when they come out, we bombard 'em with rotten potatoes. They will be blinded by the fire and frantic with stomping out the fire. I hope they sleep with their shoes on."

At that moment, I knew Witty was a genius. He could lead an army into battle just by pure bullshit, but I didn't want to be part of his plan. I like the Wicker twins. I want to be like them. I want electric lights and a radio in our tent. I like Freddy too. He is smart. He has a key to his dad's grocery store. I learned more about sex by reading yellow-paged magazines by the streetlight that shined brightly through the store window than from any other source.

“Let’s all take a break and go to your store,” Witty suggested. It’s only three blocks and there’s only one streetlight. To avoid it, we snuck down the alley. We crouched down below the huge display window facing Center Street so no one could see us, while Freddy slowly opened the screen door so it wouldn’t screech. He turned the key and we were in.

Witty grabbed *Adventure Life* before anyone had a chance to sit down.

“Listen up, guys. You ought to see what I’m lookin’ at. Here’s the cover.” He held it up, so the streetlight reflected and reflected the sheen of the glossy cover. “Wow, boobs.”

He turned his back to us, so we couldn’t see the cover.

Freddy stood up and went to the cigarette rack. “What’s your poison tonight? One pack only. Dad will notice more. Kools? Kents? Newports?”

I didn’t want to smoke. I’d tried and I thought I’d cough up a lung. Gum, candy, a sucker, anything in the whole damned store would be better than being made fun of for not smoking…

“Kools,” Witty commanded.

Freddy nodded and plucked a pack from the row of cigarette packs. "You can smoke 'em here, but don't leave any ashes. Knock 'em off your fag into the cuff of your jeans."

"Light 'em up, pussies," Witty said. "Now I'm gonna read and you better listen carefully and keep your hands out of your pockets. The title is *Are You Ready for This*?"

Even I nodded my head.

"*The Blonde Gang Moll of Africa's Jungle Bandit* is our stimulation tonight, but don't write about it in your English class." He fell back on his hunched heels and laughed.

I didn't tell Witty or Freddy, but I swiped a *Man's Adventure* magazine while everyone was intrigued by Witty's reading. *Play-girls of the Seven Seas* would be good reading with a flashlight under the bed covers.

Witty read with a low, mellow voice, "I was captured by the Amazon tribe, stripped of all my clothes and forced to lie prostrate at the feet of the voluptuously naked queen." He rolled the magazine into his hands. "More tomorrow night. If and only if we pull off this raid on the Wickers with no casualties. We can finish the story. That means, my good men, nobody gets caught. We scatter and nobody goes back to our tent. Got that, Amigos?"

He knew I hated being called Leon. I nodded. He lit up a Kools.

Leon

My Story for Creative Writing

Mom's Apple Pie

Mom didn't like me to call her that. "It's Mother. Mother with a capital 'M,'" she said to me and to my two older sisters who have long since moved out to become mothers, one having eight children who now called her mom and Theresa, who is Mother Superior at St. Mary's Convent in Winona.

Once a year, Mother Theresa invited me, Mother-with-a-capital "M," my brother who was two years older than me, myself, and my sister with the eight kids, all whiners and brats and her husband, the preacher who wished he were a priest, to the convent for Sunday dinner. Of course, it couldn't be Easter, Christmas, or any other Feast Day when she invited us to the convent. It had to be her choice, "Our Feast Day," as she called it.

Mother-with-a-capital "M," my brother and I settled ourselves into the big, black Buick. How I loved sinking into the back seat as we floated down Highway 14, up the hills and down the valleys on our way to the Mississippi River Valley. The limestone slices left by the road crews who had cut the roads made me think of dragons' scales. I counted the monsters and named them from “A” for Amos to “P” for Peter.

“Are you holding onto those pies?” Mother-with-a-capital “M,” asked. She had one eye on the road and the other on the rearview mirror. I knew she couldn’t see me or the pies. Ah, those pies. Fresh, still warm, cinnamon spice apple pies warming my lap. I looked up at the dragons as we flew by. Father in heaven, this is as close to heaven as I ever need to get.

Mother-with-a-capital “M” hit a hole in the road, a hole so big that even that old sofa-on-wheels couldn’t fail to take offense. The Buick bounced once. And then everyone and everything flew. Her hair and hat hit the car roof. My brother’s handmade Mother’s Day card sailed like a broken crust to the back seat.

I rose up and slammed down. Face, arms and Mom’s apple pie all smashed together. I licked my nose and flicked my tongue in anticipation of the taste of blood. The car had come to a stop. Its door opened and a cinnamon smile broke across my face as I tasted Mom’s apple pie and felt her arms around me. “Happy Mother’s Day,” I said.

Mom picked a piece of apple from my chin and laughed. Licking her finger, she said, “Good pie.”

My Inheritance

They auctioned her off
Faces to vase
Staring at dust
Behind cut-glass fingerprints.

"Wonder what she's worth?"
A brother bids, a sister nods
An uncle smiles
His wife buys.

I fold my shame among her handwork
Failing to announce
my need
for this last piece of her.

Ellie and Max Fremont

Author

Ellie Fremont sat straight in the oak dining chair as she gazed through the window. She fingered the rough edges of the chair's arms that were nicked and worn during the years she had been married to Sam. Terri-cloth curtains swayed with the gentle summer breeze. It was wonderfully cool for a summer afternoon in southern Minnesota. The blue and white curtains' brass rings tinkled gently. She gasped as a sudden burst of wind forced her lungs to contract. She closed her eyes to remember the scent of spring's lilac that bloomed just beyond her view from the dining room window. A sharp pain in her chest followed each breath. She lay her on the embroidered pillow on the table.

Toting a milk can in each hand, Max trudged slowly to the house. He stepped beside the back door and hoisted the cans into the cooling tank. He gasped for breath. Water oozed over the tank's edge, puddled around his boots and ran onward in tiny vein-like rivulets as it sought the dusty earth. He cupped his hand and scooped a handful of water into his mouth, all the while unaware of the excess spilling onto his shirt. Unaware of the vivid blue splatters of wet spots that contrasted with the faded blue of his jeans, he scraped the cow dung from his boots on the door sill.

Ellie raised her head and eyes from the pillow. She curved her lips into a smile.

"You okay?" Max questioned as he reached into his pocket for his pipe. "Damned pipe. Need a new one." He tossed the pipe on the table and pulled out a card of cigarette papers from his shirt pocket. Rummaging through his pocket, he found enough loose tobacco to make a cigarette. Unconcerned over the shreds that dropped to the floor, he spread the tobacco, rolled the paper, and lighted it.

Ellie coughed lightly, and clung to the edge of the chair for support. She stood and walked to the kitchen. She was grateful that Agnes Olson had been kind enough to come over during the afternoon to drop off some literature from the Women's Christian Temperance Movement. She also brought a pot roast of beef, carrots and onions. Agnes knew it was one of Max's favorite dishes. Ellie had told Agnes after church the previous Sunday that she wasn't feeling well, but she didn't want Max to worry. She confided in Agnes that the spring plowing, seeding, and ever-present milking and barn chores were wearing on Max. Thirty years farming. No children and no doctor bills. Yet, they could not get ahead. Max works hard, Ellie tells Agnes and he never touches the devil's swill.

Ellie removed the potatoes from the oven, burning the tips of her fingers slightly as she poked the potatoes to see if they were done. She pulled the roast from the oven and slowly lifted it to the table. *Max will like this,* she thought. Removing the cover, she spooned a bit of the gravy to taste. *Maybe a little more pepper. Just a pinch.* Everything was ready. Max would go to town to the pool hall to play Schafkopf for a couple of hours. Ellie would leave the dishes for morning, a practice she never allowed herself, but tonight she was too weary. She had rarely been sick during their marriage. She had thrown many a bale of hay onto the wagon and had even helped Max milk the cows before the electricity. One miscarriage, followed by a hysterectomy a week before their second anniversary, left them childless.

Max's voice snapped the air, forcing Ellie to remember where she was. "I'm getting damned hungry."

They ate in silence. Max was too hurried and too preoccupied to chat. There wasn't much left to chat about anyway. He finished his meal, belched, picket his teeth with a pipe cleaner, tossed his fork with a clang onto the plate, pushed from the table and reached for his town coat, a black denim western style with gold metal snaps. With the slam of the door, he was gone.

Tears slid from the small gray pupils, spilling over into the wrinkles time had folded on Ellie's face. Frail body wracked with pain, she coughed. Darts of pain penetrated her chest. She closed her eyes and lay her head on the table, sending a water glass tumbling to the floor. She wanted to doze off into a world free from pain, free from the coughing, free from the struggle to breathe.

Max slammed the rusted door of his Ford pickup and paused to fill his pipe with Velvet tobacco. Tobacco worked equally well for rolling as for tamping. Dull yellow glare from the streetlight reflected from the cracking gray of his pickup.

"Evening Max," Emil Olson raised a hand from where he sat.

"Max," Leonard Bierward nodded.

"Howdy," Maynard Menard tipped his hat. "Ready to play some Schafkopf?" Ray Steiner rose slowly from the bench next door to Charlie's Pool Hall. These same men had been occupying the bench and gathering for evening cards most weekday evenings. Clouds of pipe smoke swirled upward in the night breeze. The men rose nearly in unison from the bench and entered the pool hall. Max nodded a greeting to Ida Blottum. She sat in the wire-backed, steel-legged chair beside the Wurlitzer jukebox that had replaced the player piano. She wore a faded black dress with yellow sunflowers turned manila. Her brown cotton knee-high socks sagged when she stood. Ida, who drank two tap beers every evening, excluding Sunday, would sit and sip for an hour. Tonight she abruptly stood and shuffled to the bar. She didn't have to say a word. A six-pack of Grain Belt was placed carefully into her burlap carrying bag with straps long enough to hoist over her shoulder. Turning, she shoved open the door and toddled up the hill toward her little house at the south end of Main street. Freddy Selmy knew the house and her well because he delivered milk, six eggs and Velveeta cheese by bicycle to her home every Saturday morning.

Following his companions, Max shuffled past Ida toward the back of the hall. Beer cases, mostly Grain Belt and a few Pabst and Shells, were stacked against the wall. Three spittoons stood between steel-legged chairs at the card table. Two light bulbs with a brown painted tin shade hung above the table. Close to the front window, the light cast a faint glow on the words "BEER POOL CARDS" painted in white shoe polish on the window.

Light from the tiny dining room window spilled gently into the darkness. Farms can be deathly quiet and forlorn in the darkness. A branch brushing a windowpane could startle or soothe a person. Ellie coughed several times, each cough stronger than the last. She gasped. "Max… Max, I need you," she whispered. She knew he would be home in a couple of hours, but she couldn't catch her breath. She attempted to move her hands to her apron pocket to retrieve her handkerchief. Her mind spewed streaks of light that rose and seemed to explode in her forehead. She wanted to call for help, for Max, but her lips quivered. She tried not to cough, hoping to relieve the pain. While holding her breath, the room warmed like a mist on a foggy morning. She felt warmth spread through her body until she coughed blood. Suddenly she felt youthful as she stood at the altar of the tiny Methodist church a block off of Main Street. Everyone she knew and some who were unfamiliar turned their heads to watch her float up the aisle in the flowing white wedding gown.

The sour smell of sweating men, tobacco smoke in the air and tobacco juice in the spittoons mingled in the air. Six cards were dealt to the five players, with two cards placed in the middle. The Schafkopf deck consists of 32 cards with 4 Aces, 4 Kings, 4 Queens, 4 Jacks and numbers 10, 9, 8, and 7 of each suit. Each player is dealt six cards with two cards placed in the middle. The player who chooses to be "Picker" picks up the two middle cards. Discards two cards from the hand and names a card that he wants to be played as his partner. No one knows who the partner was until the call for the card was played.

Emil announced to be a picker and he named the holder of the Ace of Hearts to be his partner. After the third round, Max had to play the Ace of Hearts. Emil and Max were skillful Schafkopf players. Max kept insisting that they use its American name Sheepshead, but Leonard Bierward insisted that they keep the original Bavarian name. Beer, Bavaria and Shafkopf were inseparable, Leonard insisted. Max and Emil scored the most points during the evening. They celebrated by drinking a beer purchased by the losers.

Emil and Max chuckled. Charlie carried the beers from the bar to the table, unmindful of slopping the beer onto the sticky floor. It would be at least a week before a new supply of sweeping compound would arrive, so customers would have to put up with sticky floors for a while longer. No one seemed to care.

"Here you are, fellows. I hear you, Max and Emil cleaned up again," Charlie laughed.

"Yah, we're card sharks, we are," Emil joked as he grasped the foaming beer. He tipped the glass to his lips, letting a dribble of a beer run down his shirt into his bib overalls.

The mechanical click of pool balls pierced the lull in the conversation. Max bunched in his hairy hand three soiled paper chips printed with barely legible words, "Good for five cents in trade at Charlie's," his share of the Sheepshead winnings. He shoved them into his pocket. He pushed his chair from the table and stood, his towering body casting a bleak shadow across the plywood table littered with half-filled beer glasses and flecks of tobacco.

"Guess I'll be goin' home," Max said. "Thanks for the game and Charlie's chips."

"Night, Max. See yah tomorrow night," replied Emil as he circled his finger in a lot of beer on the table.

"Night, Max," Charlie offered.

"Yah," Max replied as he pushed through the door, letting it slam behind him.

He turned the key as the grinding sound of the starter drowned by the spasmodic rebukes of the engine. With the engine sputtering and spitting, Max backed from the curb and drove down the deserted street toward home.

As he approached home, he noticed the light seeping from the tiny dining room window. *Wonder what Ellie's doing up this late,* Max thought. *Damned odd.*

As he entered the house and hung up his jacket on the kitchen wall hook, he could see into the dining room. He noticed Ellie's small grey head drooped on the table amidst the stained supper plates. Touching and shaking Ellie's shoulder, he said, "Ellie… Ellie, wake up!" Trying to wake her, he reached for her curled hand. Clay-like warmth of her flesh created a thickening knot in his stomach that grew until it became tangled in his throat.

"Ellie… Ellie. My God! My God!" he cried. His blue eyes contracted with disbelief and pain. Beads of sweat appeared above the narrow furrows of his forehead. Spasms of heat coursed through his body. He retched and stumbled toward the door. Thrusting it open, he stumbled toward the pick-up.

Agnes Olson woke as she heard their German Shepherd Rusty barking. Emil was putting on his pajamas in the bathroom. It had been a good evening of card playing. Sheepshead, he smiled. Both heard a vehicle skid on the gravel in front of the house. Agnes pulled the cotton window curtain to the side. She saw Max stumble out of the truck. She rushed from the bedroom and clambered down the stairs, her daisy-print nightgown trailing behind, presented a ghostly picture as her bony frame descended into the dining room. Emil emerged slowly from the bathroom, muttering because he thought Agnes was having another of her night terror dreams.

Max collapsed on the wooden dining room chair, folded his arms tightly around his chest and buried his head. Breathing heavily, her face white and contorted, Agnes gently rubbed Max's slumped shoulder.

"Max… Max… what… what is it? Ellie?"

"She's dead," Max blurted.

Max functioned mechanically while Emil and Agnes made funeral arrangements with the pastor of the Methodist church. Agnes discovered a carefully written paper inside Ellie's Bible. She had listed songs she wanted to play and sing at her funeral. She had noted that these were the same songs played at her mother and father's funeral. She had written that she wanted "Abide with Me" to be sung by the minister at the beginning of the service. "Just a Closer Walk with Thee" was to be sung by the congregation at the end of the service. She had even chosen the Scripture Lesson: John 14: 1-3 and II Corinthians 8: 38-39.

The service concluded with the pastor reading a prayer Ellie had identified as her mother's favorite prayer. "Dear

God. Look very tenderly upon me this day, dear Father, and strengthen my heart with Thy love, that my hands may be strong for Thy service. Help me to follow the ways of peace and to cultivate with diligence the art of being kind. May I leave no little kindness undone while waiting for an opportunity to do some great thing!

Teach me how t give a cup of cold water in Jesus' name. Help me, dear Lord, to quench somebody's thirst, to cool some fevered brow, to refresh someone who is weary.

Teach my lips to speak words of love, of tenderness, of courtesy. Help me to do now the things that need to be done now, making the most of each golden moment as a priceless gift of love.

And all through the day, dear Father, let me serve Thee and my fellow men with joy and with a gentle hand.

In your eternal fellowship, keep us all until the morn's eternal dawn and all the shadows have fled away and we see Thee face to face, through Jesus Christ our Lord. Amen."

Platonic shadows offered sympathies and sent cards stacked up on the dining table and flowers filling the church altar. Max became haggard. Days passed without much notice on his part. Every evening before sunset, Max stood before Ellie's gravestone. Carried by the breeze, gray puffs of clouds carried by the wind wafted among tombstones, casting intermittent splashes of moonlight as Max rubbed his hand across her name.

Cupping a handful of moist earth, Max hurled it toward the tombstone blotting out her name. Unaware of an owl's screech, Max stood and walked toward the woods. Unfastening the cemetery gate, he walked toward the marsh that lay between the protestant and Catholic cemeteries. His mind reeled with the thought of her cold grave. *Her warm body, now pasty and cold, lies rotting,* he thought. He shivered as a finger of night air brushed the nape of his neck. Fog rose from the muddy shore and circled above the cattails as Max's heart thumped.

Max faced the wind, delighting in the pain as it bit his face with icy breaths. He stumbled among the soggy leaves, feeling the dampness heavy on his overall pants legs. He stumbled and felt his legs chafe.

Ellie—her face—her smile. The thin boney hands skillfully kneading dough and her warmth as they brushed his shoulders in the night rose in macabre visions as Max walked among the pines. Sweat, dripping cold from his forehead, was wiped away by the slap of branches. Pine needles stung his cheek. He pushed forward, his arms outstretched as if reaching for a form hidden in the moon-glow ahead.

A burst of moonlight emblazoned the clearing near his barn. Max's breath fell in heavy gasps. The light from the open door of his house warmed his body, forcing him to go limp with a sudden release. He walked toward the light, feeling the presence of Ellie within, and he pushed the door open. A jar of Ellie's strawberry preserves stood on the table. *Ellie's. Ellie. Ellie's,* he thought, but the slam of the screen door echoed with a note of finality telling him she was gone.

Max seized the strawberry preserves and smashed the jar against the wall. "Ellie, Ellie," he murmured as he scooped the mass into his hands, unconscious of the shattered glass as it cut into his hands.

"Speak to me, Ellie. I'll stay home tonight. We'll sit and talk. We'll have enough money for crops. Don't you worry, It isn't so bad. We'll make it again this year. New curtains. Lace. I'll buy Belgian lace curtains. And new linoleum for the kitchen. All the things you've wanted."

Max walked into the small living room. Blood dripped from his hands and he spotted the braided rag rug. He stooped to wipe a red blot with his handkerchief. Their wedding picture stood on a pine mahogany-stained shelf Max had made. Everywhere he turned, he saw signs of her love, remembrances of the years together, building, planning and hoping.

He clutched the wedding picture and looked into her eyes. Tears welled up and flowed as he spoke words he hadn’t used in years. “I love you.

Unbraiding

The folds of her neck drooped
over the couch arm-like braids
of a sagging noose.

As she tucked her feet into her shadow
her marbled eyes rolled inward
the brown cat's eye flecks
clawing at her upper lids.

His liquid voice seeps
through subconscious cracks
She has prayerfully been mortised.

Droplets of remembrance pool
harden into mirroring cataracts
reflecting all thought inward.

Scooping a handful of sleep
from the glassy end table
she crumbles comfort

into her tired mouth.

Not Much to It

There really isn't much to it.
No shock there at all.
But rather like leaves
Burning gold from frost,
Or birch logs consuming.

There really isn't much to it.
No shock there at all.
Smiles of children laughing
Well-worn books upon the hearth.

"What?" you ask.
"Oh. I don't know.
Maybe if you like
we'll call it remembering
loving, living
or dying,
perhaps.

Leon

Old folks were dying in Eyota at a rate that was alarming. I felt the need to atone for my sins. I had ridden my bike with Freddy Selmy to deliver small bags of groceries to many homes in town, to Betty Bellamy as often as I could and to Max and Ellie Fremont's farm. I loved the adventure of pedaling down the gravel road on the way to their farm while I struggled to stay in the vehicle ruts in order to avoid sliding and crashing in the loose gravel. I always had trouble keeping up with Freddy, who looked like he was flying. After attending the funeral, I went home and wrote:

Among Fallen Weeds

Gravestones claw at the dead,
finger the living
who sprinkle seed
between granite reflections.

No one sees his shadow
scraping at her name,
or thinks
to tell Him

He’s broken His commandment.
Thou Shall Not Kill.

This man,
ignoring the planting,
dreams on
of sprouting, growing
and flowering.

The dying is done
among fallen weeds,
alone
in the sacred sun
where granite survives.
He’s broken his commandment
thou shall not kill.

The Wicker Twins

After the Wicker raid we rounded ourselves up at Freddy's dad's store. If the Wickers came shouting after us at our tent, they would find it vacant. Witty warned us to stay out of the streetlight. "No more sex magazine education for us tonight," he laughed and lit up another Kools. I had to swallow my pride and admit to myself that Witty was a genius.

"We did it," Witty said. "Freddy… Freddy… Freddy… you shot off after lighting that bag of dog shit so fast I thought you were a comet."

"Too bad I didn't get to see them stomping on the fire. Good thing they still were wearing their sneakers," Freddy laughed.

"That's what me, the general gets to see," Witty blew cool smoke rings and penetrated them with his middle finger. "I was posted behind the corner of their garage. When I saw the flames, I knew they wouldn't see me peeking around the corner. You should have seen them. I'm sure you heard them curse and yelp while they stomped out the fire. And when the dog shit stench hit them, they scuffed and scraped their feet on the grass. I held my hands over my mouth to silence my roar of laughter, turned and ran."

"They were wearing new Converse sneakers," I added.

Witty and Freddy looked at me like I was from another planet.

"What?" both of them said.

"School," I said. I saw them in the halls. "White Converse."

Witty glared at me. I thought he was going to crush his lighted cigarette on my arm or face as he stood up. "You find something special about the twins wearing matching Converse sneakers?

"We're talkin' about warfare here, and you. You talk about their sneakers? What's wrong with you?" Witty tapped his pointer finger and dropped cigarette ash on my head.

"Sssh. Get down. Shut up. Don't say a word or move an inch," Witty commanded.

He saw the Wicker twins emerge from the shadow of the post office across the street on the corner from Selmy's store. I was scared. How could they know we had pulled off the raid? Why were they coming toward the store? We had sworn that we wouldn't ever tell anyone that Freddy had a key to adolescent heaven. Food, drink, cigarettes, and educational magazines! I lay flat on the floor. Witty and Freddy did the same.

I could hear my blood pounding in my ears. What if they threw something through the window that would break through? What if they raided our tents and found we weren't there? Why were we so stupid? We should have gone back to the tent. Should have been asleep in the tent. Stupid. We were so stupid. It was Witty who commanded, but they had no reason to come after us. We were friends. At least Freddy and I were friends. I didn't know any of Witty's friends except Freddy. We still had a chance. Their shadows disappeared around the post office corner.

"Get up," Commander Witty said to me. "We're gonna race back to our house. Hide in the screen porch. Run! Run as fast as you have ever run when Freddy opens the door. Freddy! You stay here. Lock the door after us."

"What? Why? Why me?"

"Freddy, listen, we're safe at home on our porch. They wouldn't dare knock on the door. And you're safest here."

Witty stuck his nose around the magazine rack and rose up just enough to see the street. He held up his hand like he'd seen John Wayne do when leading troops in combat to signal us to hold back. He dropped his hand to his side and waved me forward. I was always under his command.

"Yes, sir," I whispered.

Witty turned to me with a look that terrified me. His lips were so tight that his cheeks lifted so high they made him squint. He pointed his middle finger to his lips. I wasn't sure what he meant, but I didn't utter another word.

Freddy squeezed open the door while trying to ease the outside screened door quietly, so the scrape of its bottom wouldn't make a sound. I prayed that the tin Coca-Cola sign nailed to the middle of the screened door wouldn't make a noise.

"When I raise my hand," Witty whispered to me. "We run like hell."

Freddy was shaking.

"Freddy, you hunker down here for a least an hour," Witty commanded. "Then you sneak back home and crawl through the window to your bedroom. Did you remember to leave it open?"

"No, but I usually sleep outside on the porch."

Freddy pulled a Kool's and motioned to strike a match. Witty grabbed Freddy's wrist with one hand and crushed the cigarette with the other. "Don't you dare light up! If you can't get your ass home safely by sneaking through two alleys, you will never be a friend of mine again."

Thank God Freddy's dad never asked the next morning about the nose and lip smudges on the window. Freddy told us that his dad told him to clean the outside of the windows and didn't say more. But Freddy always feared his dad knew more than he would ever say.

Leon

I handed Freddy the shovel. "It ain't gonna be just an ordinary old snow fort. We gotta build something that we can sleep in. Maybe even find a way to put in some heat. Gotta have a sturdy roof too!"

"I've never seen so much snow," Freddy groaned as he dug deeper into the snow.

The snowplow had piled it up so high we could play King of the Mountain on top of it on the east side of our house. We couldn't see Oscar Matteson's house from inside our house. We had only dug down about two feet when Freddy heaved the shovel at me. He was breathing heavily and sweating even though it was easily below zero. Witty thought we were childish for playing in the snow. He was shooting pool with the Wicker twins at Charlie's.

"Just three more feet," I said as I picked up the shovel. I wanted the space to be as long as a coffin, wide as two coffins and five rather than six feet deep. No, I didn't intend for us to be buried in our snow cabin, but I wanted it to be comfortable, so we could sit up and lie down comfortably. I knew our parents wouldn't let us sleep in it, but we had all of Thanksgiving vacation to enjoy it. We only had this weekend before school was out for vacation. I wanted our snow cabin to be finished by Sunday, so we could use it during the break.

Witty and Jeb stopped in the street to look up at us atop the giant bank of snow.

"Well, look at what the kiddies are building!"

"Looks nothing more me than a hole. Digging your graves," Jeb laughed. He pulled down his stocking cap lower over his ears.

I kept on shoveling and tossing the snow backward over my head just to show off. I shoveled furiously. The threesome walked. Their breaths sent clouds of steam, so Witty and Jeb lit up cigarettes. No one would be any the wiser if they saw them walking down the street.

"I think we're down to about four feet," I leaned on the shovel. "Think you can handle the final foot?" I tipped over and fell into the hole. Freddy laughed and laughed as if I had told him the first dirty joke he'd ever heard.

Lest I Become Vapor

My eyes are

bees

that   limp   across   the   sky,   searching

for

flowers

crusted in

sugared snow.

I need less

of

the   crippling   snow blown   sky

and I need more

of

rainbow mists   making honey   in the sun

or

I   will

evaporate

like

pollen

dust

in

the

wind.

Peace Garden

Two months before the Memorial Day Parade, Betty Bellamy, followed by seniors Eric Sundstrom Jr., football quarterback, trumpeter son of banker Eric Sundstrom Sr.; Witty Holman, trumpeter; cymbal crasher Jeb Wicker; Head Majorette junior Heather Helgeson approached Mr. Arnoldi in the band room. There wasn't enough room in the school for a band room, so the school board had purchased P.S. 8, a one-room rural schoolhouse that had been moved in from three miles north of town. Nearly all of Eyota's 500-odd residents gathered to watch the building placed on foundation blocks behind the Eyota Community School building. Rinaldo Arnoldi, Master of Science in Music Education, Class of 1949, sat behind his desk. His lips curled around a clarinet reed; his fingers tapped the rhythm of the "Washington Post" march. His mind counted the number of parades Eyota Commercial Club had sponsored the band to march during the summer months. He was on an extended contract through the end of the Eyota Reaper's August Fest. After that, he could spend two weeks fishing at Big Gull Lake before returning to the fall term of teaching. Three seniors: Eric Sundstrom Jr., football quarterback, and band president, trumpeter-son of banker Eric Sundstrom, senior Witty Holman trumpeter Jeb Wicker, cymbal crashes, and

Head Majorette junior Heather Helgeson followed Betty into the room.

After a quick glance upward, Arnoldi lowered his eyes to the parade line-up spread before him on the desk. *Students usually wouldn't interrupt a deep-in-concentration teacher,* he thought, *and if they ever interrupted him, he scowled at them until they cringed and tilted backward on their heels.* Today he didn't feel like scowling and he didn't feel like looking up or talking. Thirty seconds became a minute. He sensed breathing. His own? A bell rang. Classes ended. Five minutes and band rehearsal would begin. He knew he couldn't avoid the entourage for five full minutes. Finally, he looked up at Betty and smiled between clenched teeth and a clarinet reed flapping between his lips. He spat the reed from between his teeth and wiped spittle from his chin with the corner of his sleeve. Belly unfolding like a great hot air balloon inflating, he stood and faced Betty and the students.

"Where are your instruments?" he questioned as he lifted his director's baton from the desk.

"Mr. Arnoldi," Betty began. "These band students," she waved her hand behind her to motion them to move up beside her. "Have a wonderful idea." She flashed her smile toward him and opened her expectant eyes widely.

You have no right to look so beautiful, Arnoldi thought. He waved his baton in front of the group in a grand sweeping gesture. "This is the idea group?" he said. "No, I won't consider buying any rock music for marching." He laughed like a great whale spouting water.

"Mr. Arnoldi, it's not that," Betty said, her voice undulating. "They are serious." As she finished her sentence, thirty-six bands-people banged through the Quonset hut doors, chattering and slamming instrument storage locker doors.

"Quiet!" Arnoldi roared. Every day they chattered and slammed their way into the band room, and every day he roared, "Quiet!" It had become a familiar routine for him and them. He had thought of tape recording the 'Quiet!' and had even done it once when he knew he was going to have a substitute teacher. He chuckled as he remembered the substitute, the petite Mary Warner telling him of their ruse. The students had chattered and slammed their way into the band room; she turned the tape recorder volume as high as it would go. Arnoldi's 'Quiet!' almost shattered the windows. The students quieted, took their seats and burst into laughter when she took the podium.

"Yes, yes," Arnoldi said. "Idea people are always serious. What is it? And make it quick. We have to rehearse. God knows we need it."

"We've made a report, a plan," Betty said. The students nodded their heads in agreement. "It's about the Memorial Day parade." Eric nudged Witty and they both grinned. Traditionally the Memorial Day parade ended at Eyota Park, but the boys had renamed it Ramaway Parking. There had been rumors about Arnoldi when he was an Eyota High School student. A folk fact or myth circulated among high school students and some townspeople this time of year. The talk was that Arnoldi had been caught breathing heavily while having sex in the back seat of his father's Buick in Eyota Park after Prom.

Witty spoke for the group. "We've been elected to decide what the band's gift to the community could be this year and we, along with our band mother, Betty Bellamy," he turned to smile at her. He continued, "We have decided to create a peace garden for Eyota Park. We need to get started quickly so we can raise money. We will buy flowers and plant them in letters to spell out PEACE."

"Here is an outline and a sketch of our plan," Betty offered the document to Mr. Arnoldi.

"I can't read it now. Rehearse!" he pointed his baton toward the chairs as if to wave them away. "Come see me tomorrow." He later read the report, liked the references to the remembrance of the Hiroshima bombing victims, liked even more Betty's joyous face, and enthusiastically recommended the plan to the Memorial Day committee. It took some hard-won negotiating on his part to get the committee to agree to try something new, but after he told them that the Rochester Post Bulletin had agreed to cover the event, the group concluded that it would be a worthwhile project.

The morning before the afternoon Memorial Day Parade, Earl Selmy swabbed the meat cleaver slowly across his butcher's apron and pulled the blade against his thigh to cleanse it. A leg of lamb lay before him, splayed and ready for wrapping. Chops he could sell, and chop he could do, and he could sell legs, hams, hocks, breasts, necks, livers, hearts, and even brains. *Good work,* he thought. Betty turned her eyes away from his. He wrapped the leg of lamb in smooth, waxed paper, punched the price and the date into the labeling machine, cranked the handle, peeled off the labeling tape and attached it to the paper. "Anything else, Betty?" he asked.

Betty ran her eyes over the bloody swath across Freddy's apron. It caused an involuntary shiver to slide up her spine.

She pressed her lips tightly together to control her surge of revulsion, uncertain if it were the blood, the steamy summer air in the butcher shop, or the sight of Earl's hairy hand grasping the brilliant white package of lamb chops that was upsetting her. "I think not," she whispered.

"Got some good chops," Freddy's father said as he wiped the palms of his hands on his apron. He yawned. "Some celebration that was yesterday. The rain held off just long enough. The radio said we will get two inches tonight after the parade."

"Umm," Betty said. "Good for the Peace Garden." She paid for the leg of lamb and turned to leave Selmy's store. That's what everybody in Eyota called it.

"You need anything else? Freddy will deliver whatever you want. No charge," he winked.

Leading the parade, the Legionnaire honor guard, composed of aged WWII veterans, huffed and puffed sweat as they marched up Eyota's Center Street. There were no street signs, but the logical name for it was Center Street. The same for Front Street. It fronted the railroad depot and the grain elevator. Earl Selmy's nose dripped and trickled into his mouth. He lapped the salt off the runnel beside his nose. "Hup, two, three, four," the fifth man called in an erratic cadence. "Hup, two, three, four." Earl Selmy hunched his shoulders to help shift the position of the flag's harness. The leather cut into the fatty folds of his back. People rose to cover their hearts as the flags passed. Many placed their hands over their hearts. Two American Gold Star mothers were given special seats with umbrellas to cover them from the sun. They stood with tears in their eyes at the beginning of the parade route

Behind the honor guard, Eyota's high school marching band blared their version of "American Patrol." Heather Helgeson, about-faced, rolled her drum major baton forward with her wrist in six forward loops and blew her whistle three times to signal the next song to be played. Strains of Sousa's "Washington Post" march uplifted the standing crowd. The drummers played louder and louder in a frenzy as if they were trying to drown the piercing sounds of Witty and his section of trumpets. Jeb clanged the cymbals. Heather about-faced once again, tipped her head backward, raised her eyes toward the sky and stepped forward down the street.

Mr. Arnoldi, the band director, had been named Grand Marshal of the 92nd Annual Eyota Old Settler's Day. Never in all of the history of the summer fest had anyone other than the mayor been named Grand Marshal. Mayor Arleigh Bjerke had been Grand Marshal for eight years running, and this was to have been his last year as marshal and mayor, but

Betty Manley had changed all that. Mr. Arnoldi rode on a hay wagon pulled by a John Deere tractor. Hundreds of potted gardenia surrounded him on the wagon. He held a four-by-six-foot hand-lettered sign in front of him. His smile appeared to have been taped to his balloon-shaped face. On the sign, gardenia blossoms had been stuck through holes in the tag board, their broken stems taped with duct tape to the back of the sign. The blossoms spelled "P-E-A-C-E."

The beer tent was soon to close. Mayor Bjerke stood talking to Earl Selmy. They stood close to the side of the tent, each holding the last cup of a long line of beers they had consumed. Outside the tent, Witty and Jeb were chug-a-lugging beers they had stolen from behind the beer tent.

Mayor Bjerke heard their laughter but chose to ignore it, remembering his own attempts at the very same Old Settler's Day rite of passage. Very seldom did he remember the sweet mixture of sexuality, the taste of beer, or the smell of Betty that had signaled his emergence. Betty Bellamy and he, here, in the park after the Old Settler's Day the August after their graduation, and he and she feared she would be pregnant, and she wouldn't be able to go on to college, and he feared fatherhood.

"Bjerke's Ramaway!" Eric's voice exploded with laughter outside the beer tent.

“Bjerke rammed a sheep in Eyota Park!” Witty’s voice added. “Hey, maybe he did it right here, right this very spot.”

Mayor Arleigh Bjerke crushed the half-empty Grain Belt can in his fist, beer squirting upward onto his face. He flipped up the bottom of the tent, grabbed Witty’s elbows, spun him around toward him and cursed, “Smart ass kid!” He lunged at Witty.

Jeb grabbed Arleigh and restrained him. “Smart ass kid! You need your ass kicked.” He backed away, picked up the beer can and threw it at Witty.

After Sunday services at the Methodist church, Betty caught up with Heather. “Would you like to take a look to see how the Peace Garden fared after all of the rain?” Heather was disappointed that Witty hadn’t been in church, but he had been unusually quiet the past two weeks after Prom. He had been polite when she gave him the silver eagle and chain as a pre-graduation gift, but he seemed distant.

Betty and Heather kept their eyes closed to the ground to avoid puddles as they approached the Peace Garden. All of the beautiful purple and yellow zinnias had been pulled from the ground and tossed in a pile. Both gasped and threw their arms around each other. “Oh my god!” Betty fell to her knees. A cloud slid by the sun. A small glint of light amongst the mud caught Heather’s eye. She bent close to the ground and scooped away the mud to discover a silver eagle. It was the chain and eagle she had given to Witty for graduation.

Witty

Morning after the attack on the Wickers' tent, I got up late and walked down to the creek. Freddy and Leon had no idea that the twins and I were friends. How they couldn't know in such a small town as Eyota attested to their naïveté. Me and the Wickers met at the second railroad bridge, where we hid our cigarettes. The second bridge was bigger and sturdier than the first and third bridges. And besides, the first bridge was too close to the depot and the third bridge was too far away. A week ago, we walked to the third bridge to pick up iron railroad spikes to use for our tent stakes. Each one had a slanted head, so they were easy to hammer into the ground. Jeb complained. He thought we were stealing railroad property. J. W. and I just laughed.

I was waiting for J. W. and Jeb at the first bridge. We always walked the rails to the second bridge where we stashed our cigarettes and beer stolen from the Witty's parents. The Wicker twins and I always balanced on a single rail while we walked from the first railroad bridge to the second. It wasn't much of a creek. It was so shallow that frogs were easy to catch. We challenged each other and tried to trick each other into falling off. I always won. "Look," I'd holler.

"Turd." Jeb would turn his head and lose his balance.

I laughed, "Don't pick it up. We'll find toilet paper not too far down the tracks. We had to get away from the nerdies, Leon and Freddy. I'd bet my life on neither of them ever having a girl more than a friend. I prayed that my brother Leon and Freddy would never find out they were at the bottom of my totem pole of friends."

While we walked back toward the second bridge, I told them that I had overheard Freddy and Leon last night after supper when they were in the tent. I was outside winding up the water hoses and they were talking pretty loud. Talking about having some fun by pulling up your tent stakes while you were asleep. I was sure they were just talking. We were too chicken to do anything after dark. I should have run over to your house to let you know what I heard, but Dad insisted that I finish painting the inside of the screened porch. By the time I was done, I thought Leon and Freddy were asleep in the tent.

"You heard them?" Jeb said. "You heard them plotting?"

"You didn't warn us. Why?" Jeb rubbed his hand over the blond buzz of hair his mother would not let him grow long. I never understood how twins could look so much alike. One sprouted blond hair and the other black, but both had curly hair. Weird! We should have nicknamed them Sunny and Blackie or Salt and Pepper.

I leaned back on the porch cushion we had stolen from the hardware store's outdoor display. "Well?" I enjoyed the moment more than cigarettes. I paused, took a long draw on my cigarette, blew smoke rings and swallowed. "I want you guys to beat the crap out of Freddy and Leon. They'll never know how you found out about the attack. And…"

"And what?" Jeb chirped as they pretended to inhale their cigarettes.

"You'll have to come after me when I'm with them. Do some pro-wrestler moves on me after you've pounded on them."

"Wow," the unison twins shouted.

I knew then that I could command them to do everything and anything I could dream up. I dropped a tiny frog from the lunch sack I had tucked inside my shirt.

J.W. and Jeb poked at the defenseless little creature. They laughed.

"Cute." Jeb rubbed his pointer finger over the frog's head.

I pulled my Swiss Army Knife from my jeans pocket. “Here!” I stabbed Jeb’s eyes with mine. “Jeb, this is your chance to prove to me that you have guts.”

“Whoa? What? What you talking about?” J. W. twisted his t-shirt neck as if he wanted to choke himself.

His eyes opened so wide you could see the whites.

He stood, his hand twisting his t-shirt tighter and tighter. He stomped his half-smoked cigarette. His eyes were so big I thought he was going to hit me. “Whoa.” I leaned back into the stolen cushion. “Relax, I know both of you and Jeb have guts, but you have to prove it.”

I sensed the approaching of a train. We leaped up and rushed to the tracks and leaned our ears to the rail while we put a hand next to our ears. We felt the rail’s vibration but heard nothing. “Get back,” I commanded. “It’s coming. I know it’s coming. Jeb?”

“What?” JEB was staring straight down the track toward town as if he could see beyond the horizon. “I can’t see it, but I know it’s coming.”

Jeb laid his ear on the rail. “I can hear a little hum.”

I didn’t like to be outsmarted by anybody—anybody ever. “If you think the train’s coming, put a penny on the rail. Then run down the track as far as you can and put your ear on the rail. The penny will derail it. And you will be the bravest little beaver in Olmsted County. If the train doesn't derail, I'll pick up the squish that was you. Deal?"

"Deal, Jeb?" and Jeb nodded.

"I'll do it, too, Witty."

"We know we can do this."

The sound of the train exploded down the tracks before any of us could say a Hail Mary or Holy Mother. Jeb and Witty knelt and wobbled their heads onto the track. I heard the screech of the whistle as it passed the Eyota depot. They are gonna die! My God! They are going to die! I grabbed their hair and pulled them into the squash of mud and muck as quickly as we could to escape the derail. I knew the derail would never happen.

Together we rolled from the tracks through muck and goo into the creek. Splashing into the creek, we slid between instant death and the train's clatter-echo as the beast roared, smoked and sped down the tracks.

Dazed. We crawled hand and foot up the rocky slope and then banked the rails. We watched the caboose disappear as it passed the Eyota depot. I noticed something shiny and flat-lying among the cinders alongside the railroad tracks. I picked it up and shouted. “Look, guys, It’s the penny. Flat as a dead toad. Ain’t it pretty?”

Severings

He came today,

the owner of newborn calves,

To fix barbed strands

severed in clovered grass

To spade-scrape glass,

cracked chrome, gasoline soak

In earth dark safety.

"I will not help

nor will I mourn.

I've chipmunks, squirrels,

wrens and jays who feed

without fear.

They die," I said

Nodding with the wind surge.

Bending to his task.

Eyes hand shaded.

He looked to the sun.

Glass buried.

Fence repaired.

Spade in hand.

He looked at me.

“Done,” he said.

Methodist Church

Sunday, we sat in separate pews in the Methodist church. J.W. and Jeb are in the front row. No mother. No father—just the two of them. Witty, Mom, Aunt Neddie and me sat in the fifth pew far to the right facing the pastor.

"Leon," Mother whispered and nudged me. She leaned close to me. "Stop scratching your nose. Look at the Wicker twins. They sit quietly. Why can't you be more like them? Their folks raised them to respect the Lord even though they don't attend services. Sit straight."

Aunt Neddie spat on her lacy handkerchief. Folded it to a corner and swabbed it across my cheek. "Sssh. The Reverend..."

No one knew or even suspected that I listened to the Reverend. I knew that she was old and had been called to our church because the call for a preacher and pastor for our tiny church went unfilled until she came. Retired but not tired of religion, she came to us. I listened and believed when she read from the Bible: (Luke 6:37-42; Romans 14:1-12) "Judge not, and ye shall not be judged: condemn not, and ye shall not be condemned: forgive, and ye shall be forgiven: give, and it shall be given unto you; good measure, pressed down, and shaken together, and running over, shall men give into your bosom. For with the same measure that ye mete withal, it shall be measured to you again."

The thing that struck me the most was when the lay lady read, "Give, and it shall be given unto you." That made sense. Give? I can give Witty my trust. I can give Aunt Neddie my pledge never to drink. I can give. I can always give to try, try to be truthful.

The lady preacher continued without pause. This from the Gospel of our beloved Lord from the King James Bible, I admonish you and challenge you to go and do for the good of your soul and the lust of God who anguishes for your soul in the name of His Son, "Therefore all things whatsoever ye would that men should do to you, do ye even so to them: for this is the law and the prophets. Amen."

I whispered Amen, not knowing what it meant.

We stood and sang:

"Lift high the cross, the love of Christ proclaims,
Till all the world adore His sacred Name.

Led on their way by this triumphant sign,
The hosts of God in conquering ranks combine.

Each newborn servant of the Crucified
Bears on the brow the seal of Him Who died.

O Lord, once lifted on the glorious tree,
As Thou hast promised, draw the world to Thee.

So shall our song of triumph ever be:
Praise to the Crucified for victory."

"God bless you and keep you," roiled in my ears. I looked at Witty. He smirked. The front-row twins rose and turned to Witty as they raised their hands in some kind of strange victory. What had he told them now?

Row after row, we shuffled ourselves down the aisle, past the little annex for overflow worshipers that was never filled except when the hungry-for-bread who came to communion fourth Sunday of the month grabbed several cubes of Sunbeam bread cubes and took a long sip of Welch's grape juice.

I thought I understood the message of "Do unto others" when Mom, Aunt Neddie, Witty and I tripped down the steps to the street. It took me years to unravel what happened next.

There he stood. Stood with a sign, he unfolded in three parts. "God bless you and keep you. I am homeless. Will you help? God bless."

I looked into his eyes. He was no older than Witty. His eyes glistened. *Christ,* I thought. *Christ is here.* I stopped and reached for the search of the last coins of my allowance.

Aunt Neddie grasped my arm. "No." That's all she said.

Witty laughed at me. Mother pulled me away.

Did I care about the offering in church? Sometimes yes and sometimes no. Most of the time, all I remembered was the Sunday school offering song: "Dropping, dropping, dropping. Hear those pennies fall. Everyone for Jesus. He will count them all."

Mom and Aunt Neddie didn't know that I kept my seventy-five cent allowance for myself and didn't put any of it in the offering plate. I looked into the young man's eyes and I saw pain. I saw what I felt when Witty laughed at me and called me a klutz. I saw the Wicker twins' smirks when they saw me and Freddy walking and talking together in and out of school. I saw Aunt Neddie's glistening eyes when she swooned with her love of Jesus.

“Here.” I clutched my three-quarters in my fist so no one would see. I cupped his hand and handshake the coins to him. He smiled and said, “Bless you.” We turned away.

Lost in a Crowd

Fog slipcovers are orange,

black-cracked basket hoop

Mist worn in blue-green street

light.

Nureyev arching,

he crooks arm and leg

Perfecting hook shots

Swish

Swish

Swish

Rattling, ragged netting.

brain crouched behind the brow

sweat, calisthenics;

brain glory crouched behind

sixteen victories in a row.

Agile feet, arms, and hands glide

amid roar of town folk.

Slick news prints his name

in Adonis bold.

Swish

Swish

Swish

Fog slipcovers chalk

black-cracked blackboard

Dust worn in grey-green school light

light.

Socrates arching,

he crooks arm and leg

Perfect geometry

Swish

Swish

Rattling ragged reasoning.

brain crouched behind brows

lectures, college degrees;
brain glory crouched behind
sixteen wins in a row.
Agile feet, arms, hands glide
amid roar of rhetoric.
Slick news prints names
in Platonic bold.
          Swish
                    Swish
                              Swish

Wickers' Revenge

Witty and the Wicker twins met behind Charlie's pool hall near the burning barrel. Witty had talked Freddy into swiping a pack of Kools for him from the grocery. Freddy was eager to please Witty now that he and Leon were combat buddies. He and Leon looked up to and yet feared Witty. He suspected Witty was already drinking more beer than he should. Could a kid become an alcoholic from drinking too much before he even graduated from high school?

The Wicker twins had tossed their white Converse sneakers into the garbage because they smelled after they put them on before wiping off their feet from the dog dung. Their mom was always eager to give in to most of their wishes as long as they didn't become demands. She had previously purchased red and black converse sneakers in Rochester simply because she liked the colors. She also knew that she could convince the twins to coordinate the colors with blue jeans and striped pullover shirts.

"What's the plan for revenge on Freddy and Leon?" Witty blew a ring of smoke.

The twins knelt next to Witty as he squatted on the gravel. Patrons rarely parked behind Charlie's. There was always plenty of room in front for the bench sitters as well as automobiles. Charlie even placed a spittoon next to the sidewalk bench. Cigarette ashes were merely flicked onto the sidewalk and butts were extinguished with a twisting motion of the bottom of a boot. Charlie always swept up the ashes and butts every evening after closing. He emptied the spittoon twice a week.

J. W. and Jeb shrugged and looked at each other.

"What? You mean you don't have a plan? What are you? Chicken shits?" Freddy stood and glared down at the twins. "You just gonna do nothing after what they did to you? Unbelievable!" He started to turn to walk away.

"No, no, Witty. We just don't know what to do. Are you sure they did it?" JEB said. Both stood. Jeb stared at his feet.

"Here..." Witty tapped the pack of Kools on his wrist. He pulled out two cigarettes and offered them to the twins. "Here," he said. "Let's figure out this revenge thing. I know Freddy and Leon are planning to hook up a light one of those bulbs in a wire cage like you see mechanics us and haul in an air mattress for the tent this afternoon. Leon told me about it. He was smiling from ear to ear. All I could think of was what you two might do to them for revenge."

J. W. cupped his hands around his cigarette as he lit it, drew in his breath and inhaled. Jeb hesitated before lighting his. He didn't want to look like a loser. He closed his eyes from the sting of smoke as JEB exhaled. It was a big deal for JEB to look manly whenever he was around Witty.

Witty looked at Jeb while he hesitated to light his cigarette. He knew Jeb wouldn't inhale, but I didn't say a word. "Here," he said. "Let me light that for you." Witty put Jeb's cigarette in his mouth and pressed it against the glowing end of his. He puffed and handed it to Jeb. Later, in high school, Jeb pretended his need to piss when he slipped out of the Ford parked in the hayfield. He emptied his beer onto the ground along with his piss.

Witty talked the Wickers into a night raid on Freddy and Leon's tent, much like, but more intense that had been done to them. What had been done to them was merely horseplay. Commander Witty wanted this raid to be a bit more spectacular. One that Freddy and Leon would not forget. He would tell them that he was going to stay overnight with Eric Sundstrom, who would be elected football captain in his senior year.

"I have a great idea," Ricky bent over to whisper in the twins' faces. "Rather than beat them up, why don't you sneak up on them around midnight? Your folks never check on you while you are sleeping out, do they?"

"Nah," JEB said. "They trust us. Always have."

"Good and here's where we get lucky. It'll be pitch black tonight because there's no moon. They won't be able to see a thing when they turn out the light."

"But what about us?" Jeb asked. "We won't be able to see either."

"Flashlights. Hold them like the cops do. You keep them pointed on the ground and don't make a noise. Here's where it gets fun," Witty puffed up his chest. He was in command again. Chaos and no consequences.

"Their bikes will be lying on the grass beside the tent. I guarantee it. You must be quiet like the stealthiest navy seals all of the time. Be careful not to make a sound. Put down the kickstands and park the bikes side by side in front of the tent. I'm sure the flap will be closed. Leon's paranoid about mosquitoes."

"I think we can pull that off, but what's next?" JEB was excited. Jeb was silent.

"Well. I want them to feel more panic than you. I've got a stash of cannon salutes and some punk that Leon doesn't have a clue about. I keep them in a cigar box under my bed. Punk is much safer than a match or a lighter and you can use it from a greater distance. You will have to be quick to make this work," Witty continued.

"Make sure you light the punks behind the garage, so nobody sees the match flare while you light the punk." Witty went on to flesh out the plan while JEB lit up another cigarette and Jeb coughed from the smoke.

That evening Witty told his parents that he would be staying overnight at Eric's house. He said they were going to go over some plays for fall football. Freddy and Leon had hooked the light to an unused shepherd's hook from the flower garden. They wouldn't have to spread a blanket on the ground to put their sleeping bags on. The inflatable mattress covered most of the ground. What wasn't covered at the head of the mattress was a perfect place for pounding the shepherd's hook into the ground. Everything was perfect.

Freddy brought a bag of circus peanut candy, chocolate mint cookies from the bulk cookie bins at the store, a six-pack of Dad's root beer and a new edition of "The Devilish Urges of Pastor Richesson." They ate and drank and giggled as they took turns reading stories from the magazine. Freddy's dad kept them under the counter rather than in the magazine rack with the romance, sports, muscle-building magazines and Look and Life, among others. It was great to have electric lights, but Leon's mother had warned that 10:00 meant lights out or there wouldn't be any sleepover the next night.

A lone mosquito had buzzed into the tent through the half-inch unzipped tent door flap at the very top. "Dammit," Freddy said. "I should have known better. I know how you hate the little pests." Freddy crawled across his open sleeping bag and tightly zipped the door flap. "No more will get in." Freddy felt and heard the buzz of the remaining nuisance as he stood and turned off the light.

Both he and Leon scrunched into and zipped their sleeping bags. The mosquito buzzed Leon's ear. Slipping his arm out of the sleeping bag, he waited for the noise. *Whap. Slap.* "Damn. I missed it."

"Hunker down in your sleeping bag and cover your head," Freddy suggested.

"But I won't be able to breathe. One more close encounter and I'm going to sleep in the house," Leon said. He heard a loud slap from Freddy.

"Got it. I think," Freddy said. After neither of them breathed in silence, they said good night and zipped their sleeping bags up to their chins.

Witty had no intention of going to Eric Sundstrom's house. He went to the twins' house and hid in their tent until they had finished supper.

"Hey, what are you doing here?" J. W. flashed a big smile. Jeb carried a portable radio and strawberry shortcake dessert their mother had insisted they take to the tent for a snack.

"I couldn't let the troops carry out their duty without the commander," Witty chuckled. "Besides, I had to deliver the cannon salutes and the punk, or the mission would have been incomplete. And you will need someone to light the punk while you two are pulling up the tent stakes."

At a quarter to twelve, Witty and the twins slipped out of the tent into the dark abyss. "Flashlights?" Witty asked. "I brought one. That's all I could find in the garage when I left."

J. W. whispered to Jeb. "Did you get ours from the kitchen drawer? I told you, Mom keeps a couple of flashlights and candles in the bottom drawer." He reached out and squeezed Jeb's arm.

"Ouch," Jeb said loudly.

"Ssssh," J. W. and Witty whispered loudly.

J.W. released Jeb's arm. "The flashlights?" he said a bit too loudly.

J. W. pulled a flashlight from his jeans pocket. He pointed it toward the ground and turned it on. He shined it at Jeb's face. Jeb grabbed it and turned it off.

The three clasped hands. “What do we do now?” Jeb asked with a quiver in his voice.

“Give it to me!” Witty hissed. He pointed it directly into Jeb’s face. Turned and lit up J. W.’s face. “Looks like you guys need a commander. Follow me.”

When they reached the back of Witty’s attached garage, they stood in total darkness except for the fading beam of the flashlight. Witty shook it. “Dammit! You sure picked a great tool to light up our plan.” He shook it again and it shined a little brighter. “I’ll stay here and light the punk. You two take the flashlight and sneak over to the tent. Pick up each bike and throw them on the entrance. Then run like hell. Get out of here. I’ll light the fuses of the cannon salutes and throw them as close to the tent as I can, one right after the other. Go!”

Jeb focused the light just a foot or two in front of his feet. From behind. J. W. put both hands on Jeb’s shoulders. He wanted to dig in tightly to be certain he wouldn’t lose his grip, but he tried to relax his grip. Jeb tripped on a garden sprinkler, but he didn’t shout or swear. He bent down to rub his ankle and J. W. squatted with him, hands still clinging to Jeb’s shoulders. Jeb shrugged his shoulders and whispered fiercely, “Let go. We’re almost there. Sssh.” They were so close to the tent that they could hear someone rustle around inside. Stunned, they knelt beside the tent until the noise stopped. Jeb heaved one bike and then the next above the zipped tent flap. Screams erupted, cannon salutes exploded. One followed quickly by two, three, four.

The Wicker twins flew by Witty as each salute lit up the sky. Later Witty would be reminded of the combat scene when he was crawling in the sand with live tracer bullets streaming overhead during basic training. He wasn't scared now. He was laughing as he threw the last cannon salute. In the flash of light, he heard Freddy and Leon screaming and saw two bikes rising in the air and falling again back onto the tent. He ran just as he saw the light go on in his parent's bedroom.

The bike pedals and handlebars punctured the tent fabric. The light bulb shattered and the portable radio's plastic cracked. Freddy and Leon unzipped their sleeping bags. They couldn't see anything in the dark. Not knowing which way to turn, Freddy scraped his head on a bicycle pedal. He reached with both hands and tore a hole around the pedal. He ripped and ripped the tent fabric as though he were sinking in quicksand or drowning in Fremont's marsh. He climbed out with Leon close behind him. A bright light seared his eyes.

Eyota School Grades 1-12

Leon

Freddy and I were lowly 10th graders and Witty and the Wicker twins were seniors. There were 32 students in the senior class. Our class was a little bigger with 39 students. Eyota School seemed normal size back then. Classrooms were built around an inner gymnasium with a stage at the north end and two classrooms at the south end. First graders occupied the first-floor room on the east side of the gym, with grades 2nd, 3rd and 4th continuing on the east. West of the stage, the Industrial Arts' room was located. I don't remember what else was on the west side, but the 5th and 6th grades were combined in one room at the south end of the building, right next to the dreaded office.

Junior and senior classrooms, home economics, the library and science rooms were all located on the second floor. Lunch tables were set up in the west hallway in a long line. We could go home for lunch if we like. Freddy never went home because his parents worked in their store. Mother made me pack a lunch every day except when they were serving Sloppy Joes. Cora Fuchs made the best-tasting Sloppy Joes in the world. Years went by and I was still hungry for the flavor. Witty, the Wicker twins and a few girls and guys who smoked hustled down to Charlie's. His wife put in a hot dog machine just for them. And neither she nor Charlie cared if the kids smoked. It was harmless and probably made them feel more grown up.

I wanted to play trumpet, but after a few weeks of futile effort, my tone still sounded like farts. I gave up on music right there. Never touched another instrument in my life. The Wicker twins were a different story. They both played trumpets and were the darlings of band director Mr. Arnoldi. I swear that he featured them in duets during every in-school concert. I never went to any of the evening concerts, but I suspected that they were featured there too.

Freddy and I learned how to inhale. We didn't like Kools, so we settled for a much milder Kent's brand. I think Freddy's dad might have known that Freddy was sneaking a pack now and then. But I know for certain that Witty was paying for his cigarettes. Freddy told me that he always put the money in the till.

Witty and the Wicker twins never spoke to Freddy and me during school, but that was okay. We didn't have any of the same classes. Sometimes juniors and seniors were placed in the same classes like physics and higher algebra. Freddy and I were required to take

Biology is like every sophomore in the state. Witty talked to Freddy only when Witty gave money to Freddy for cigarettes. Usually, Witty caught Freddy by the shoulder while meeting in the hallway next to the biology lab. The next day, Freddy would meet Witty in the same place to hand over the "fags" as the cool kids like Witty liked to call them.

I don't know why, but Witty was the pet of mathematics teacher Mr. Knutson who loaned his aging Mercedes to Witty for Prom.

Prom

Junior Heather Helgeson was elected to chair the Prom Committee. Leon Holman and Freddy Selmy were also elected to the committee. Eyota tradition held that the junior class chose the Prom theme, planned the Junior-Senior Banquet and decorated for the Prom to be held in the Eyota gymnasium. Several meetings and discussions took place beginning in late fall. The most important decision was the theme. Everything would fall into place much more easily once the committee agreed.

Heather was a strong leader and had been popular with her schoolmates a year behind her and the seniors. She was a head majorette and was certain to be Homecoming Queen in her senior year. Blonde, blue-eyed, five foot four with a sweet and demur smile, she often dressed in a tight skirt with a discretely open-at-the-neck cotton blouse. Marilyn Monroe look-alike. She had begun dating Witty Holman during football season. Neither Witty nor Heather knew that Leon and Freddy were jealous, but then again, many young men were envious and disappointed. JEB and Jeb, along with Eric Sundstrom Jr.

Freddy Selmy was a popular choice for the committee because his father owned the town's only grocery store.

They sold more than groceries and meat. It wasn't exactly a dry-goods store, but they did stock items such as nylon stockings, rick-rack for sewing, sewing patterns, greeting cards, magazines, crepe paper, birthday balloons and candles. They also offered red stamps, not the more common green stamps, as rewards for purchases. Filled booklets could be traded for prizes listed in the Red Stamp Catalog as well as assorted dolls, dishes and pans on display in the store.

Leon had persuaded Freddy to propose "Blue Moon" as a theme. Being a good friend, Freddy agreed, but he wanted something a little more exotic. "Treasure Island," another voice suggested. And another raised a hand and a timid voice recommended, "At the Hop." As chair Heather was, according to parliamentary procedure, supposed to refrain from making suggestions. She was to lead discussions and finally ask for a vote. "These are all great suggestions," she smiled. The bell for first-hour class and homeroom rang. The meeting ended without a vote.

The next meeting wasn't held until early April. The school had been canceled for a week in March during the basketball tournaments.

"We have to make a decision soon. There is the banquet to plan and decorations to be decided on," Heather said.

Someone taped an anonymous note in my locker this morning. Heather read:

Dear Prom Committee:

Several of us, both juniors and seniors, met after school yesterday. Since we have not heard about a decision being made about a theme, we suggest "Oriental Gardens." It's different and exotic.

There was no signature.

"We have no way of knowing if this note is from a single person or a group," Heather said. No one other than Leon, who sat next to Freddy, noticed Freddy fidgeting with his pencil.

"I like it," Leon said. Other members of the group nodded and voiced their agreement.

"I do, too," Heather said. Her mind was already whirling with ideas for decorations. They needed to create something that would involve the entire class. Even though not everyone would have a date for the Prom, every member of the junior and senior class was expected to attend the banquet the Friday before the Prom.

Betty Bellamy, the class mother, was invited to help plan the menu for the banquet. None of the students had a clue about what to do. She also arranged for National Supply

Company out of Sioux City, Iowa, to print three-by-five-inch folded cards with Oriental Gardens printed in pseudo-oriental lettering and a drawing of a garden with oriental lanterns hanging from a tree.

MENU

PINEAPPLE-ORANGE JUICE

HAM

MASHED POTATOES

CARROTS AND PEAS

GELATIN MOLD

BUTTER AND ROLLS

COFFEE ORMILD

VANILLA WAFERS

SHERBET

JUNIOR COLORS

Ice Blue and White

JUNIOR FLOWER

Lily of the Valley

JUNIOR MOTTO

"Today We Follow,

Tomorrow We Lead."

SENIOR COLORS

Pink and Silver

SENIOR FLOWER

Pink Carnation

SENIOR MOTTO

"Not the End,

But the Beginning."

It was a tradition for the junior class to prepare prom decorations for the Junior-Senior Prom. Spring baseball didn't attract enough spectators to put on bake sales. The junior class had held bake sales after basketball games in the winter to provide funds for Prom decorations. Since Eyota didn't have a field big enough to host eleven-man football, there was no opportunity to hold bake sales in the fall. Moms and one or two Dads prepared the baked goods offered for sale after every basketball game. Sales were excellent and one hundred percent profit helped the coffers grow. This was the first year enough money had been raised to pay for a four-piece band and a rented mirror ball. Selmy's Shop and Save had donated punch, crepe paper streamers, balloons and boxes of pink Kleenex.

Mottled light reflected from the mirror ball spinning in the Eyota gymnasium. Witty wiped sweat from his forehead with his left hand, grasped Heather with his right and swung her around in a wide circle. Her legs flailed beneath the full pink skirt with a fitted bodice Betty Bellamy had made. The skirt required a stiff crinoline undergarment. Her legs looked like they were entangled in a cloud of tulle. Luckily, Betty had sewn in the crinoline so it did not slide down when she fell. Betty looked up at Witty as he eased her gently to her feet. She laughed.

Witty escorted her to the stage to the punch bowl's Hawaiian Punch and 7-up mixture. After drinking all of his cup of punch, Witty walked Heather to the back of the stage to share a discrete kiss. His cup of empty. Heather was still nursing her. "Drink up," Witty urged. Reaching into the inside pocket of his tuxedo jacket, Witty extracted a pint of blackberry brandy. Looking around to be certain none of the chaperones were on the stage, he said, "Here," as he uncapped and tilted the bottled toward her cup.

"No," Heather said. "I don't drink." She faced Witty as if to share another kiss, but it was actually to shield him from the dance floor and the chaperones.

Witty poured vodka into his cup and gulped it down. Poured another, drank and poured another.

Heather touched him gently on the wrist to try to stop him from taking drinking another.

"Love you," he said. He capped the bottle and stuffed it into his jacket pocket. "I've got an unopened fifth in the trunk for later."

Heather pressed against him like a flower between pages. It was nearing the end of the night. The band cranked up the volume as more and more dancers gathered on the gymnasium floor close to the band. Chaperones stood nervously nearby with their backs against the wall.

The eight-foot pink pagoda stood to the right of the punch table. Juniors had gathered after school and early evenings at the Dover elementary school to stuff pink Kleenex into chicken wire holes. They hadn't given much thought as to how they would transport it to the Eyota stage once it was finished. Fred Selmy came to the rescue. He asked the bread deliveryman if he would be available after his route to load and drive the pagoda to Eyota. The Sunshine bread man was happy to help as Selmy was a valuable customer.

Trying to keep his feet in time with the music, Witty gyrated faster and faster. Witty's wild eyes, wet brows, and perspiring palms all began to frighten Heather. She pulled away from him while all of the dancers stopped to admire Witty's one-man dervish.

Ryan Knutson

A sudden thud followed by voices, giggles and nervous chatter rapped me out of my nightmare. Crushed fenders, torn seats, and fragments of glass rattled in my head as my conscious mind intruded briefly on my nightmare. I wanted to close my eyes, so I could see the faces. They were smeared with blood. Shattered glass shards glittered in their hair. Opening my eyes, the subliminal glow of the digital clock awakened me. 3:13 AM. Louder thuds, giggles and chatter lifted me from my bed into a jogging suit.

Loud pounding, not knocking on the door, started me once more. I opened the door. "What the hell?"

"Party time!" Witty dizzily oozed through the door with Heather weaving behind him.

We had made a bet in my match class. Witty was my top student, one of the best I had ever taught. His tenth-grade brother was smart but nowhere nearly as smart as Witty. Witty had become more and more cocky as he scored one hundred percent on six consecutive tests.

"I'll loan you my car on Prom night," I had said in half-jest and full haste. "If you can score 100 on the final."

"You're on," Witty grinned, his oily brown eyes glistening.

After having made out the test weeks before the bet, I was confident that Witty and certainly no one else didn't have a chance in hell of scoring 100 percent. In fact, I took the test myself before making a bet with Witty. I made two minor mistakes. No one hundred percent for me. I think I liked Witty so much because he mirrored my own cockiness when I was his age. And I suspected there was something smoldering beneath the surface that he felt, but he could not or would not articulate. If he is like me, the ember was a nagging suspicion that he really wasn't as good as his grades in all of his classes indicated. There might be a small tear in the fabric of self-esteem that needs repair. Dare I tell him that the tear will keep ripping each time he falls short of perfection, that he will invent new and devious ways to hold back the ripping. I hoped I was wrong.

After the Prom, chaperones gathered at my apartment for an end-of-the-year party. They drank frequently and fully from 11:30 to 1:00, when they dispersed, fatigued and a touch drunk from wine, liquor and end-of-the-year ennui.

"Go home." I pointed my finger toward the door. "Go home." It was futile. Witty opened the door and a splash of bodies spilled into the room. The Witty twins staggered in with their dates. "Out!" I shouted. No one was hearing.

Heather pulled me aside. "We can't go home," she said as she pointed to Witty. "I got them this far…" her voice trailed off to a thin whisper that I barely heard amongst all of the laughter.

Witty hoisted a remaining bottle of flat champagne he had lifted from my glass coffee table. He wobbled. I prayed he wouldn't drop it. I watched as the bottle slipped from his unsteady hand just as he tipped it to swallow the dregs. Nearly tripping over the table, I lunged and caught the bottle in mid-air. Witty giggled, "Oops... slurry." Before I could take the bottle out of harm's way, Witty was sipping on a silver flask he had carried in his tuxedo pants pocket.

Gyrating his knees in slow circles, Witty threw his arms around me and started to wilt. The silver flask slipped from his hands. His arms went limp as he slid to the floor.

"How much? How much booze?" I said to Heather.

"Just that," she pointed to the silver flask draining blackberry brandy onto my beige carpet. "And that little bit of champagne."

"Lies," I snapped.

I looked out at the thirty-two Eyota soon-to-be graduates, their maroon mortarboards and gold tassels swaying with their nervous movement. They sat on folding chairs facing the stage, where I was standing behind the podium. Parents, brothers and sisters, relatives, friends, and high school faculty sat behind the graduates.

"Tonight, you begin a new journey," I began. Witty sat in the second row. Most of the class was looking at me. Witty was staring. I thought he looked defiant. I should have tried harder to reach out to him, to talk to him about his future. I was certain he would be going on to a four-year college, probably not private. Winona State was a short drive away. I should have encouraged him to apply. On the last day of school, Heather told me that she wasn't looking forward to her senior year. I asked her why. Teary-eyed, she sniffled that Witty had joined the army. I continued, "This journey you will take as young adults seeking to discover the universe of promise that lies ahead of you. I want to read a poem that I wrote for you." I knew they would be surprised to think that a mathematics teacher would write a poem.

Hold Fast

To families

Whose windows mirror sons and daughters
each child reflecting pieces
of a mother's smile
gestures of a father's hand
seen in a daughter's wave
sounds of long-forgotten voices
echoing from the backyard sandbox.

To rituals

Easter eggs dipped by purple fingers'
in rainbow-colored dyes
Christmas tree needles injecting carpets and
barefooted heels with piney perfume
Baptisms, birthdays, weddings
forever floating white and fleecy in our minds.

To disagreements

Brittle twigs snapping apart
as thunder roars
icy granite steps, too slippery to be climbed
Mud tracked across newly waxed floors

To reconciliations

Pebbles glistening beneath translucent waters
edges of clouds rubbing a sunset's ribs
fringes of leaves sheltering nests from winds

To farewells

Children swallowed by buses, homework and friends
The dawning and dusking of light
slipping through our fingertips
Graveyards to small to hold
centuries of living

To loving

Spring's melting of winter's last ice
Summer's of earth, wind and sky
Fall's flutter of grouse wings shattering the sky
Winter's warming of flaming wood

Hold fast to this, your graduation day. Hold fast.

I looked up. I noticed a glint of silver as Witty raised a concealed flask to his mouth.

Narrator

It's time for me to intrude on the characters so that I can clarify or embellish a few things. I began to realize at this point in the Eyota Stories that you, the reader, could not possibly be interested in all of the 500 hundred characters' stories about life in Eyota. So I chose a few to tell their stories. Also, I have woven in some poems that characters wrote and a few that I wrote. You can skip them if you like.

Hayfields and Shivarees

Hayfield: From Merriam-webster.com

"A field where herbaceous plants and especially grasses or legumes (such as timothy or orchard grass or alfalfa) are grown for hay."

Shivaree: From findmypast.com blog

"The traditional hazing of our newlywed ancestors."

Fall was the best time for teenagers to gather around a keg in harvested hay fields. There's even a town in southern Minnesota called hayfield. It's a town very much like Eyota (pronounced EE YOH TAH, not EYE YOH TAH). High school and junior high school fans who rode Eyota school busses to football and baseball games to competing schools often sang, "Yah oughta. Yah oughta. Yah oughta go to EE YOH TAH HI. Football, baseball, and basketball too. Come on, team, we're rootin' for you. Oh! Yah oughta. Yah oughta. Yah oughta go to EE YOH TAH Hi."

Carloads. Yes, carloads of the most daring of Eyota's high school populace and sometimes interlopers from Dover spread the word about a keg party in a hayfield not too far from town yet far enough away, so the noise couldn't be heard at the farmstead. The safest parties took place in farmers' hayfields whose son or daughter knew their parent would be gone. In all the years of hayfield parties taking place, as far as lore has it, none were ever busted. Where the keg came from was never discussed.

Hayfields were also great places for lovers to “park” and, as the old-timers would say, “spark.” Park and spark.

Shivarees were always noisy and held late at night during good weather, normally after eleven o’clock, when it might be assumed that the newlyweds were in bed. Most weddings occur in summer months or early fall. Friends and neighbors gathered with pots and pans to bang on. Hand held horns to blow, car horns to blow and firecrackers to light; the louder, the better. The ruckus would continue until a light would go on in the bedroom. When that happened, the roar became more intense until the bride and groom would appear in the doorway. Laughter and cheers erupted as they came out to fill their mugs from the keg. Shivarees occurred rarely but often enough for some Eyota High School, students to sneak in among the noise and drunkenness to help themselves to as many beers as they could drink.

Witty

He hadn't told anyone about his plans to leave Eyota just days after graduation. He needed to get away. Playing at being an athlete and student was wearing him down. He wanted to be a commander and have others follow him and his orders. Just like Leon and Freddy had done... and the Wicker twins. He had so much pent-up energy he knew it couldn't be released in Eyota (E-Y-O-TAH-HI). Never. He loved Heather. Waiting around for a whole year until she graduated? No.

He contacted army and marine recruiters in Rochester without anyone knowing. He scored 94 on the Armed Services Vocational Aptitude Test (ASVAB). Recruiters preyed upon his ego by encouraging him to enlist and apply later for Officer Training School. He signed up for induction on June 6.

JEB was the one person Witty told of his plans. He and JEB planned to go to Winona State College to room together. Both had been accepted. Witty's ACT score of 29 made him a Presidential Scholarship qualifier. All he had to was to show up for a formal interview after graduation. JEB wasn't far behind with a composite of 26. Buddies forever. Both received one hundred scholarships from Eyota PTA, enough to pay for first-semester tuition. Jeb wasn't interested in going to college. He had always wanted to be an electrician.

Witty didn't know how to tell Heather and JEB that he had no desire or intention to go to college. He admired Jeb because he had chosen a clear path. He loved both of them, but the lure, the dream of becoming a marine, was constantly on Witty's mind—leading troops, commanding and deserving respect.

Witty pulled into the field road that ran alongside Max Freemont's hay field. Alfalfa was thriving. Witty opened a Grain Belt beer. Reached across the seat of his father's '59 Mercury to hand JEB a bottle. Two more beers... three. Both were burping loudly and stepping out often to piss after turning off the dome light. Sliding back into the driver's side of the cavernous black and pink leather bench seat. Witty extended his hand across the expanse between them...

"Hey?" JEB scrunched his shoulder closer to the passenger door.

"Sorry."

"Don't be! I'm sorry," JEB said as he sat up straight.

"I didn't mean."

"I know, buddies. No need to explain."

Witty tuned the radio to WLS. The sounds and lyrics of *Michael Row the Boat Ashore* played.

"Michael row the boat ashore, hallelujah
Michael row the boat ashore, hallelujah

Sister help to trim the sails, hallelujah
Sister help to trim the sails, hallelujah

Jordan's River is deep and wide, hallelujah
And I've got a home on the other side, hallelujah

The river Jordon is chilly and cold, hallelujah
It chills the body but not the soul, hallelujah

Michael row the boat ashore, hallelujah
Michael row the boat ashore, hallelujah

Michael's boat is a music boat, hallelujah
Michael's boat is a music boat, hallelujah

Michael row the boat ashore, hallelujah
Michael row the boat ashore…"

Witty turned the volume loud enough to drown words between him and JEB Song ended. "Why don't you enlist? They guarantee we'd be on the buddy system through basic." Witty opened another beer and chugged half. "Imagine throwing grenades. Both of us are expert marksmen! Both of us commandoes!"

JEB stared at the blackness beyond the window. He didn't speak for an uncomfortably long time. Witty started the engine, punched L on the dashboard, burned ruts in Freemont's hayfield and sped off toward Eyota.

Witty dove up to Heather's house on Saturday after Prom.

Heather

Heather, Leon and Freddy had been best friends during primary school. All three were free every summer to just be kids. You won't find many parents mentioned in the Eyota Stories. The reason? Most of the characters, including the narrator, didn't know what the term "helicopter parents" meant. No one was actually neglected, but one might call it benign neglect. Kids were safe in Eyota. Nothing bad had ever happened to any child. Everyone knew everyone in the entire town. Most fathers worked at jobs outside the house and most mothers worked at jobs inside the house. Kids roamed outside and spent many summer days in unsupervised play.

Heather's parents' backyard provided the best location for kids to gather.

Heather, even in elementary school, had a unique talent for organizing games, activities and people. It seemed that something exciting was always happening or being planned. Every other week, kids gathered at Heather's to decorate their bicycles. Freddy provided red, white and yellow crepe paper streamer rolls from his dad's store. The girls wove it between bicycle spokes and made streamers to attach to handle bars. Boys wrapped crepe paper around the handlebars and clothes-pinned playing cards to their spokes. They pretended they were riding motorcycles as they speeded up and slowed down to vary the sound. They paraded around neighborhoods. Traffic always stopped for them when they rode, sometimes eight or ten single file down Main Street to Eyota Park.

On other occasions, Heather planned, directed and performed in plays staged in her backyard. Leon provided the main stage curtain and his cowboy-print double bedspread. He hung it on the clothesline. Most of the fun in planning a production was in the search for props and costumes. Heather created a list and offered to buy a chocolate malt for the first person that could guess the title of the play by reading the list.

1. Black dirt.
2. Water.
3. Wagon.
4. Dog.
5. Glitter.

Heather didn't want to make it too easy for them and the other classmates or friends who would make up the crew, extra actors and part-time audience when they were "on stage." Maggie asked Leon what he thought. Leon asked Cheryl. Cheryl asked Freddy. No one even had a guess.

Heather admitted that she had made it too difficult, so she said she would ask her mother to take the cast and crew for milk shakes or malts after the performance. Everyone was excited.

Heather ran her fingers over the liquor stains. Cigarette smoke still clung to her Prom dress. She had hung it in the back corner of her closet. It would have to be dry-cleaned, so she could wear it again next year for her Senior Prom. Her parents were not poor, but they were frugal. Her mother had agreed to pay $50.00 for the dress of Heather's dreams at Three Sisters in Rochester. She stumbled on a box at the bottom of the closet. Bending down, she picked up the white child's dress she had decorated with Elmer's glue and silver glitter for one of her roles. Beneath the dress, a tattered cotton dress smeared with mud, along with a blonde wig, fell to the floor. She felt tears welling. *The play.* It was many years ago when fairy tales came true.

A week after Prom, Heather was still angry at Witty for his excessive drinking. She refused to sit near him during study hall during the fifth hour. He, JEB and Jeb's buddies walked the three blocks to Charlie's to drink pop, smoke cigarettes and eat hot dogs. She apologized to Mr. Knutson after math class just before noon lunch. Witty overheard her as he rushed by her toward the classroom door. He banged the door shut.

Earlier in the morning, just before the first bell rang, she caught up to him by his locker. She touched him lightly on the shoulder, but neither of them spoke. His locker was such a jumbled mess; he cursed when he couldn't find his English Literature book. Heather held back the words she needed to speak.

Witty graduated with a 3.0 GPA. He hadn't told anyone that he had enlisted in the army and would be leaving for basic training at Fort Bragg, North Carolina, two weeks after graduation. Beer wasn't strong enough for him to buck up his courage this night. He had drunk three Screwdrivers before he stopped at Heather's house. He planned to tell her about his enlistment. Neither of them could have foreseen that Witty would not return home for eighteen months, ten months of silence after basic training.

Witty spread out his father's army blanket under an oak tree in Eyota Park. A silver cross hanging from Witty's neck glistened in the moonlight. He planned to offer it to her as a pre-engagement commitment. He wanted to be sure that she would remain faithful to her during her final year of high school. Maybe he would make enough rank to marry and return with her to wherever he was stationed. Witty kissed her and reached to unbutton her blouse.

"Please, don't," Heather said.

Witty was confused. Words had never been spoken between them about commitment. He lay back on the blanket after Heather refused to have a drink of vodka.

"How can you drink that straight?" she touched his face. "I wish you wouldn't drink so much."

He sat up and laughed. "You won't even let me touch you and you lecture me about a few drinks?" he scoffed. Tipped the bottle to his mouth and gulped so much that vodka ran out his mouth onto his shirt. "God dammit!" He pulled his polo shirt over his head and wiped vodka from his mouth.

Heather began to shake. Moonlight seemed to spotlight Witty. He drew himself up on his knees and fell upon her as she tried to sit up. She had never seen so much anger on his face. He swore at her.

"I'm through with you. And this goddamn town. Find your own way home."

Witty stumbled on the front door threshold. I hoped our parents wouldn't awaken. I slipped out of bed and met Witty reeling in the hallway. He mumbled, "You can have." He belched, “Can have her.” His lips were so tight that his cheeks lifted so high they made him squint. He pointed his middle finger to his lips. I wasn’t sure what he meant, but I never uttered another word about that night.

Steiner

A late October wind blew cold. Steiner stepped outside his butcher shop/locker plant doorway next door to Earl Selmy's Shop and Save. Steiner stocked bread, milk and a few canned goods. His principal income was derived from butchering and storing meat. He and Earl Selmy had agreed to close their stores at 6:00 PM and open at 6:30 AM. Oak leaves from the lone tree on the block skipped across his feet. He was tired, hungry, and bored. Maybe some of the guys would be at Charlies'. He rubbed his elbow; it ached. Still not far enough from war to heal. He paid little attention to the shuffle of the figure bent under a black umbrella as it passed his doorway

Steiner raised the bottle of Old Grand-dad Bourbon to his lips. Swigged and wiped his lips with his sleeve. Charlie didn't have a liquor license. He only sold domestic beer. Auto headlights brushed across Steiner's legs. He watched the red taillights smear in the rain as they faded away. The subtle hiss of the tires spraying water soothed him. He ran his fingers over his baldhead. His hands had personally killed and butchered two Holstein steers that day. Leaf fat caked under his fingernails. He curled his stubby fingers and raised them to his nose. Scrubbing with Lava lye soap scoured his hands but couldn't cover the smell of blood.

Ida stopped to adjust her umbrella in front of Selmy's Shop and Save. Her house was an Eyota curiosity. Few people other than Ellie and Max Fremont had ever entered Ida and Jacob's house. Local boys and sometimes girls mowed her lawn, shoveled her walks and often delivered a camouflaged six-pack of beer to the porch fronting three sides of her hexagonal house. Ida and her late husband, Jacob, had designed the house. Everyone called it the Blottom house. Jacob and Max Fremont had been best friends up until the day Jacob died. When one entered at the back of the house, a small bank of pine cupboards lined the walls of the triangular entry. All rooms faced a center opening with doors leading to a room with a sink, hotplate and an oil-burning stove. Two larger rooms served as a bedroom and living area. A toilet commode was walled off in the corner of the living area. All of the rooms had no ceiling other than the exposed rafters. Ida had waited too long for the rain to stop before leaving home to walk the two blocks to the store for milk and bread. A Closed sign dangled sideways from the door window. She folded her umbrella while standing on the post office corner, a half-block from Charlie's Pool Hall. She had overheard chatter at the post office that the EUB church was hosting an evangelist that afternoon. She hoped the rain would keep him and the people at home. She had forgotten to ask Charlie to send someone to deliver a six-pack.

He whispered in her ear, "Praise the Lord. Repent all ye sinners and let the blood of the lamb wash away your sins."

"Bloody Christian," Ida muttered before. "Where are you?"

He stepped around the corner into the lone streetlight. "Repent!" he shouted in her face. "Repent and let the blood of the lamb wash away your sins."

"I ain't no sinner," Ida said calmly. She shook the water from her umbrella, wrapped the tab to secure it, and pointed it at him. The wind blew and she wiped a droplet of rain from her forehead. Charlie's bar sign blinked.

She sat down in a wire-legged chair near the table where Max Fremont and his pals normally played Schafkoph, smoked and drank tap beer. The wind picked up and splattered raindrops against the window. The steady tap, tap of the rain, along with a glass of beer, reassured her that she was not a sinner.

Steiner slammed the door. "Nasty night out there, Charlie." He wiped the rain from his baldhead. I see you finally put in that hot dog machine the high school kids were begging you for."

Charlie nodded his head. "Yeah, since they like to rush down here during their thirty-minute lunch break to smoke. I thought they should be able to buy something other than potato chips to eat."

"Looks like there won't be any card players coming in. Sure wish you'd stock some good German beer," Steiner said. He nodded to Ida. "You want a cigarette?"

She laughed, "You see that preacher man down there by the post office?"

Charlie slid a glass of tap beer across the table to her. A little of the beer sloshed on the table. Ida looked up at him with disgust.

"Preacher man? No, didn't see a soul," Steiner said. "Did you go to the afternoon session at the UB church? I had fewer customers, so I thought you might have seen some of them there."

Ida lifted the glass to her lips. Sipped and wiped the back of her hand across her lips. "Nope. I'd never go to one of the revival meetings. Would take them too long to save my soul."

Steiner sat down beside her. He tipped his glass of beer to her.

"I'd like to see that. You at a revival meeting."

A face pressed against the rain-streaked window. He remembered the man, didn't know his name. German—he was sure he was a German from the fields years ago. Treated the Kraut prisoners too well. Rapping his knuckles on the window until he caught Ida and Steiner's attention, he shook his fists and hissed, "Sinners." His face dissolved in the flow of water rushing down the window.

Ida sighed. She liked Steiner. She recalled that it was in the fall, while she was away in Minneapolis studying shorthand, typing and clerical work, when she first met him. She had come home for Thanksgiving. Maple leaves blazed in the afternoon sun. Unusually warm for November in Eyota. Now and then, it snowed and laced the leaves with brilliant-white with snow. He stood behind the counter in the meat market. She thought his English was too perfect. It seemed practiced, somehow. Nobody in Eyota spoke so perfectly without a hint of some kind of accent—German, English, and occasionally Norse or Swede

Ida didn't know when Steiner had arrived and had begun working at the meat market. No wife. No family. Just Steiner. She guessed they were close to the same age.

Steiner touched her hand.

She moved hers away.

"Ida? Are you foreign?"

"No, why?"

"Your face is familiar."

"Lived here all my life. My grandfather had some German prisoners of war working on our farm during the war." She took a long swig of her nearly empty bottle of Grain Belt.

"Charlie," Steiner said. "Zwei beers."

Witty Returns

Eyotans become caught up in a rush of preparing spring gardens, cleaning the house, worrying about too much or too little rain and paying taxes. Everything seemed quite normal. Early Selmy hadn't raised the price of sugar or coffee. Bread and eggs had gone up just a penny since New Year's. No real crises or interesting events seemed to be on the horizon.

Ida Blottom bustled into the post office to pick up her afternoon mail. She clacked across the tile floor and tugged at Betty Bellamy's sleeve. Betty was a bit annoyed when she dialed past the final number that would unlock her post box.

Ida's American Gothic lips framed her words, "I saw the Holman boy, the one they call Witty, toting an army duffle bag on his shoulder and carrying a suitcase in the other. Didn't think he'll ever get over Leon and Heather."

"Last I heard," Betty said. She snapped open her post box and ran her hand around to make certain it was empty. "Last I heard when I asked Leon. He said Witty got in some kind of trouble in the army. Something about an entrenching tool, but I didn't know what that was. Leon shuffled his feet and looked at the ground. Turned and walked away."

Ida's mouth drooped like her brown cotton stockings. "Why do you think he's back in town? I thought he might be going overseas. Was gonna make a career in the army."

Ida took hold of Betty's arm as they stepped across the street to Selmy's Shop and Save. She thirsted for a beer, but that would have to wait until after supper when fewer people were out and about. "Afternoon, Earl," she said.

"Afternoon, Ida and Betty." Earl nodded his head while inserting a paper roll into the adding machine cylinder. He cranked it a couple of times. The paper popped up. He tore it off and tossed it into the wastebasket beneath the sales counter.

Ida stood on her tiptoes to open the dairy cooler. Barely able to stretch her arm far enough, she grasped a one-pound carton of Land O Lakes butter. She handed it to Earl. "Please cut this in half. You know, a whole pound spoils before I can use it up. And wrap me six summer sausage slices. Set the slicer on four."

"Four?" Earl looked at Ida quizzically.

"Two," Ida stammered. "No, no, I mean four."

"Are you sure? I always set it on two for you."

“Today, I want it on four. I’m hungry.” She eyed Betty, who was testing the firmness of a tomato with her thumb. “Don’t slice your finger and get blood on my sausage.”

Earl didn’t care to ask her what was making her hungry. He sliced the meat, wrapped it neatly in white butcher paper and sealed it with masking tape.

“Say, Earl, did you see Witty Holman walking down the sidewalk a few minutes ago?”

“No, I’ve been busy.” He heard the screen door scrape against the sidewalk. Without looking up, Earl knew it was Sam Gorman who shuffled his feet from the sidewalk on the wooden floor. “Sam,” he said. “Same?”

Sam nodded his head and pointed to the stack of Copenhagen chewing tobacco stored in a tin tower next to the cigarettes.

Earl pulled one can from the bottom opening and a click followed when the next can dropped into the cylinder.

Sam opened the can, withdrew a respectably sized chaw and tucked it in his cheek.

Ida tapped Sam on the shoulder to encourage him to step aside. She leaned over the counter to peer at Earl. “The bulk chocolate mint cookie bin is empty. All I see are crumbs. Nobody’s gonna buy those.”

Ida never bought chocolate mint cookies. Always wanted her summer sausage sliced on number two and a pound of butter cut in half. Fred couldn't recall Ida ever buying anything but molasses cookies, either. Four at a time.

"Sorry, Ida. I didn't notice that the bin was empty. I'll order some tomorrow."

"Never mind. Four molasses cookies will do just fine. No, make it a half dozen. I'm hungry."

Betty placed a load of Sunshine white bread and a quart of milk on the counter. "I'll walk you home, Ida," Betty smiled.

"Fine, but I'm still wondering what the Witty boy is doing at home. I thought we were overseas or something," she repeated.

After tucking her groceries into her cloth bag, Ida turned and ran squarely into Heather Holman. She and Leon had been married the summer after their graduation.

Leon

Written after mother died

Worms and Flowers in Silver Bay

Mother's nurse telephoned about the blood pressure pills I had forgotten to deliver. I told her I couldn't leave the shop because the fish were biting, and if I didn't keep the worms cool, they'd die. Tomorrow's the end of fishing season, anyway. Then I'll lock the doors and bring the pills. She hung up on me.

Bill dangled a worm between his fingers like a twisted telephone wire.

"No, I don't understand why the house has to come down," I said.

"Progress, Don. That is what it is." He pulled another worm from the carton. "Dead," He said.

I shivered, feeling his voice slide down the inside of my legs.

I don't fish. It's not because I wouldn't if I could, but I make my living supplying the bait. Sometimes I think I'm the stream, the stream with no end, beginning or middle, but I'll take care of that. When wormy hooks are thrown, I won't splash. I'll babble underground where no one will see me pulling hyacinths into the ground. I'll drown lifeguards sent from Alice's Salvation Army Band. Her son bangs the bass drum; her daughter blows the tuba in concert for fathers they do not know. I am no Hyacinthus. I pollute the bay.

Alice is a hook. "You really should drive up and take the kids fishing, Don," Alice said. She adjusted her bra strap with her little finger coiled under the swatch of fabric slithering over her shoulder to her breasts. Her eyes snagged mine. *Half-sister,* I thought. And what is her other half, a piece of poison liquefying in the heat between us?

"No, no I can't. Too busy. Maybe this winter, we can ice fish."

"It would be good for you to be with the kids again. We need a man around."

Greasy words, I thought. Her forefinger curled over Bill's hand as he lay his palm on the display case glass. I saw their hands shatter. I was kneeling on the broken glass, trying to piece them together. My knees were bleeding.

Crazy? Yes. Crazy quilted from 1940's fabric scraps, American made, indeed, but cleansed from the soap residue rinsed out of Mrs. Johnson's sheets. The taste of Mother's washings is still on my tongue. She hated dirt and cats. She said, "Be thankful you are a man. None of that cat dirt will stick to you." That was before I was old enough to smell cat dirt.

"He's dirty," Alice had said years ago. Her hair looked like carrot peelings because of the peroxide she had dumped on it.

"Who?" I asked.

"You're so stupid. You're a ten-year-old dummy." She wiggled in the sunlight.

"At least I don't have carrot-peel hair!" I threw dirt at her, but she didn't care. She was twirling a minnow in the sun in front of my face.

"Bill's dirty," she giggled.

Alice wore a habit of dress-up clothes. I sensed her nakedness underneath. Bill washed his feet in public, even dried them on Alice's habit. He called her his pussycat. When mother heard that, she said we all had dirty feet. Ever after that, I washed mine twice a day, but they always got dirty again.

Mother's feet weren't dusty often anymore. She planted hyacinth bulbs along the fence. While she was digging a hole to plant another bulb, she looked up at me and said, "I think I'd like you to call me Mrs. Johnson from now on." She smiled, gently nestled the bulb into the earth and covered it with her hands

This afternoon a bulldozer will knock over Mrs. Johnson's house. Her tombstone is on the front porch. I bought it in case the blood pressure ceased to work. Years ago, I cut myself on her picket fence. The scar maps a course through the groin. Alice doesn't know that Mrs. Johnson sleeps in the basement of Peeler's Rest Home. She doesn't know I bought her tombstone. Yesterday is too long ago for her to remember. I remember there was pain in my groin. Hyacinths won't help.

"Got any plastic bait?" Bill rubbed worn dirt on his trousers. The muddy streaks left by his fingers looked like claw marks. Alice had the smell of him caked under her fingernails. Mrs. Johnson screamed at me to wash my hands.

"I can't... I can't. The dirt won't come off. It won't come off any of us." I felt paws on my shoulder as I slid to the floor. Paws without claws lifted me.

I heard a voice from afar calling, "Don? Don?"

I stood. The clock's second hand piled up debris behind Bill's head.

Dead worms float in Silver Bay. Mrs. Johnson's illegitimate son pollutes the bay with dead worms. Alice plants hyacinth bulbs and laughs. Now she wears black negligees as her dress-up clothes. My half-sister plays with the Salvation Army Band. Who prays for me?

"Call a priest! Call a priest?" Alice's hysteria bubbled through my thoughts. I had fallen into a box of carded fish lures and plastic worms. I laughed between clenched teeth. Bill held my shoulders in his hands.

Bill ran up and down my spine with cleated boots when I was a kid. I enjoyed lying prostrate on the rug, and with my nose buried, I smelled Bill's feet, the feet that had sneaked through the dew to my mother's door. But I shriveled from the smell of him on her hands when she washed my mouth. Mother kissed me then. That was before I climbed the picket fence. I bought her tombstone, but he'll run up and down it with his cleated cat, knocking down her house and crushing her. Who's dead?

"Here, drink this." Through a sloshing river slopping against glass banks, I saw Alice's body rooted in the ground. A hook snagged her for a moment, then swirled away. I hadn't known that I was a hook. My hands reached to replace it. She would flourish there, seeded and watered, transplanted in cat dirt. The bait cards wouldn't be sold. I couldn't send them for Christmas. Tomorrow I'll have to pack them away for winter.

Tomorrow is the end of the fishing season. Alice smells of live worms and flower pollen. Mother and Alice baited the hooks that hung between their breasts. I saw them swinging behind the fence. I climbed over. They knew I would slip on the dew. Bill understood the blood seeping into his hand, but he's never seen my scar. He's fishing in Silver Bay. He'll never know I've polluted it.

I ordered a father from the 1952 Sears catalog. Mother laughed and made up a story for me. She said he was hanging in the Louvre. He was really driving a cat, but I didn't know that. I didn't know what the Louvre was either, and I couldn't figure out why father was hanging there or what he was hanging from. Alice told me I didn't have a father and could never have one. I dumped worms in her lap and she laughed.

I went to the library and searched for the Louvre. When I found it, it looked like a monumental tombstone turned on its side beside a muddy river. Mrs. Johnson must have seen that too, but I didn't want to think like her. I wanted to call her mother instead, but she insisted on Mrs. Johnson and nothing else. The house smelled less often of cat dirt then, but some mornings I thought I saw marks on her face. Red spots lifted her cheeks higher than usual and her eyes seemed to swim in a furry mist.

"Lift him up."

Tomorrow the doctor's nurse will call to say that Mrs. Johnson's blood pressure exploded an artery in her heart. I'll have killed her because I didn't weed her garden and I let her hyacinths die. Bill will understand the blood running from her mouth into his hand, but he'll never see my scar. He understood the watering of hyacinths, but he could never see why I wouldn't weed them. I told him the weed-ing was a waste of time because dust and worms would win in the end. He climbed on his cat, his sweaty face frosting the garden.

I should tell Alice about it tomorrow, but she'll want to bring flowers if I do, so I'll just remind her it's the end of the fishing season. After that, when the sun drops over the horizon like a rock falling into dry grass, I'll wait for the bare-boned moon to smear its skeleton over the stream. I'll bait my hook with a chip from Mrs. Johnson's tombstone, and we'll go together to fish in dusty water while hyacinths flower in the dirt by Silver Bay.

Mrs. Johnson's nurse telephoned about the blood pressure pills I had forgotten to deliver. I told her I couldn't leave the shop because the fish were biting, and if I didn't keep the worms cool, they'd die.

Burning Barrel

Eyota has no curbs, gutters or street signs.
No garbage collector either.
We burned trash in rusted oil drums,
sort of an outdoor public airing of our indoor lives.
I returned on my first college Thanksgiving
to strut what I had become.
Purple and gold pennants fluttered from my suitcase
I watched for neighbors' curtains to open just a peek
as I splashed through slush toward our corner house.
I saw mother through the garden gate,
staring out of the smoke.
Envelopes took on butterfly wings,
My high school romance
burst into flame
A red envelope lifted a foot above the flames
and stepped to the ground.
Mother had found my kindling point.

A Story by Leon Holman

1986

The Cursor

There must be a story here, somewhere. Two more cigarettes, one more glass of brandy, three more scratches of my posterior and I'll begin.

"Ass. Now there's a word!" Ronald Windgate settled backward into the antique swivel desk chair, exhaled a wine-laden puff of smoke and smiled. He typed "Ass" and stared at the blinking cursor. He swiveled the chair to where he could see the plump goldfish swallowed in water and staring walleyed at Ronald. "There must be a story here, somewhere." Ronald stared back at the fish.

Yesterday he had sat with the Rotarians at their weekly 12:15 luncheon meeting. Actually, he had been invited to deliver a fifteen-minute speech on creativity and its relevance to the businessman in today's teeming world of commerce. He had given the speech, hadn't he? He remembered Salisbury steak with mushroom sauce sloshing around in his stomach while he tried to speak without belching. He remembered the high school diver who was "Athlete of the Week" who sat to his left. He was too shy or too embarrassed to lift a fork.

The kid nearly tipped his chair when he slid it from the table. Ronald wanted to ask him if his ass was as sore as his. He wanted to ask him if he knew about babbitry, but the kid was escorted away by the gray principal in the gray suit who drove the gray Pinto.

So Ronald returned to his computer, where he stared at the blinking cursor and the word "Ass." A *Sports Illustrated* commercial echoed in the hall from the family room television. "Subscribe by calling 1-800-555-5555 now and you will receive a second complimentary copy of our celebrated Swimsuit Issue." Ronald blinked at the cursor. Deleted the period after "Ass" and replaced it with an exclamation point. "Looks a bit like a sperm attaching an egg," he mused. "Or does the egg attack the sperm?" He deleted the sperm and egg and replaced them with a period.

"Ass, I Ronald. Thirty-eight years of fat," he typed. "Ass. Get your knees off my chest!" *There is a story here,* he thought. Maybe that damned blinking cursor will stop hypnotizing me.

"You big, hairy beast. Get offa me." Poor little Richard fought against wrists, ankles and feet that pinned him to the baseball field's dusty infield like a beetle in a display box.

"Pull it out! Pull it out!" Whitey chanted. Chucky joined and pressed hard on Richard's arms to hold him down.

The sharp, onion-like stink of sweat seeped into Richard's nostrils. *Whitey's hairy chest might smother him,* he imagined. Bubbles of spittle collected on Whitey's upper lip. It all seemed to happen in slow motion and would happen over and over again for years to come. A bubble of slobber oozed into the corner of Whitey's mouth. A string of spit dropped its own weight onto Richard's face. He struggled to turn his face to the side and felt his neck crack.

Ronald saved the file. He didn't know where the story might take him. All he knew was that he needed to get away from the blinking cursor. Needing something stronger than wine, he opened the desk drawer. He liked his Korbel brandy neat–no ice. He turned the cap on the bottle and poured more than needed into a green glass tumbler.

The cursor continued blinking as if to say stop-go, go-stop repeatedly. He slammed his fist on the desktop. Spilled brandy leaped into his open journal, puddle on top of the hurried scrawls he had made five months before. Hurriedly, as if whisking away a dead fly, he swiped away the brandy with the cuff of his shirt. Beneath it, he read:

January 14

January's calendar has a hole in it. You've let it happen again. Now, swear, this is the last time. Finish!

Ronald licked the rim of the brandy glass, set it beside the journal and filled the glass to the brim. *Glass Ass,* he thought before lighting a Winston cigarette. He sighed, opened the saved file and highlighted the entire file. Cigarette smoke stung his eyes. Brandy soothed his sore throat. All it takes is Command X and it all disappears. The cursor blinked at the end of the word *crack.*

Closing his eyes for a moment to savor the flavors of tobacco and brandy, he sensed that he could finish it.

"We're gonna pull it out, you little wimp. We're gonna pull it out. We're gonna pull out your lonely, little chest hair and you'll never grow another one."

Richard felt a sharp sting.

"Look at this, wimp." Whitey held the hair between thumb and forefinger before Richard's eyes.

All weight lifted from Richards's chest and arms as he lay flat on his back. Whitey danced and laughed around and around Richard while chanting, "Wimp. Wimp. Wimp."

How many bottles of brandy and how many packs of cigarettes will it take for me to get to the end? Ronald blinked at the cursor. He swirled the brandy round and round again, entranced by the beautiful glow as he held it close to the computer screen. *Rose might have been prettier,* he thought. *But maybe not.* The cursor might destroy the beauty. He lit a cigarette, inhaled deeply and exhaled a cloud of smoke that billowed around the computer screen. He closed his eyes, so he could imagine the next scene.

"Not one more pack, Whitey. I ain't sellin' you no more packs of cigarettes." Richard said. He squeezed his fourteen-year-old old buddy's crisp dollar bill in his hand and shook it at him.

Whitey grinned at him, "You'll wonder where the yellow went when you brush your teeth with Pepsodent" He smiled, "Come on, Richard. It was just a little joke pulling out hair."

Fact or fiction?

They were fourteen. Ronald saw that moment stretching out in his conscience like a rubber band taut between opposing hands. Would it snap back and sting one or both? Was this the way to the end? Thirty-eight years old and still feeling what he felt then? He returned to the cursor.

"Yes, you will. You will sell me a pack. You will sell me cigarettes for as long as I want 'cause you are a wimp. And I'll tell your dad about what Mrs. Dolder made you do." Whitey said.

Richard handed the crush-proof box of Newport Menthol cigarettes to Whitey. Richard felt fat wearing the white grocer's apron his father forced him to wear. He felt fat and greasy because he perspired in the August embarrassment of his young life. Felt guilt because he had lied to Whitey about Mrs. Dolder coaxing him to pull down his jeans and underwear in her laundry room. He had told Whitey every detail he could recall from reading pulp magazines from the store magazine stand and Whitey had believed him.

Richard and Whitey had been best friends ever since meeting in Sunday School when they were six years old. They had been instructed to memorize Bible verses to recite it in front of the entire Second Baptist congregation.

"Stand up straight and smile," Richard's mother shoved him from the pew. Whitey had said his "piece" perfectly while flashing his perfect teeth shimmering in his angelic smile.

"And in those days, there were shepherds tending their flocks by night..." Whitey performed flawlessly.

Richard stood perfectly straight. His back to the altar, he stared into a black hole of memory—a hole so deep there was no going to or coming from, just blackness swallowing him.

He awoke from the black hole of suffocation to the scratch of starched sheets scratching his buttocks. He opened his eyes to the smell of lilac.

"You embarrassed me and everyone in the church by not speaking your "piece." Pastor Rathborne insinuated that I had not taught you properly. He said he doubted if you would ever learn the Lord's Prayer!" Richard's mother stood over him with a hand scrub brush in her hand.

"You've sullied your soul. Roll over. I will scrub you clean of your sin."

Ronald saved the file under Cursor Finish.

Thirty-eight years of fat growing between my ears created a larder of my very own imaginings. My name is Richard Desmond—not Ronald Windgate. I wrote **The Cursor.** So, even though I have always answered to the name Ronald Windgate, I know I am Richard Desmond. Author of numerous short stories, poems, a novel and contributor to The **Eyota Stories.**

Notes from Witty's Journals

September 12, 1971

I have been promising myself that I would record army experiences. I prefer not to call them memories. I worry I might repress the bitterness. How do I record listening to Dwayne, the twenty-year-old grunt, who told of sitting on his parents' backyard steps in Compton, California, with his hand filled with orders to report to Fort Lewis for transport to Vietnam.

He survived 365 plus a few days in the infantry. With a fifth of Seagram's gin and a quart of orange juice in hand, he plopped down on the end of my barrack's bed. I had arrived the day before being transferred from Fort Hamilton to Fort Holabird. Dwayne poured a half-fifth of Seagrams into the orange juice carton. We shook it and drank while he talked. He lit a joint and stared at me.

I didn't know anything about him or Vietnam. Had he killed? And what have I done? I don't think I can ever see beyond my fears and what they can do to my soul. I'm trapped here, waiting for orders, not knowing if I have to get a ride on Flying Tiger Airlines.

Dwayne inhaled as he handed me the joint. We drank and smoked. I mentioned Flying Tiger airlines. He said the cargo planes carried 200 passengers and about 5 flight attendants. They flew in replacement troops and flew home the wounded or Gis like Dwayne, who had survived 12 or 13 months in-country. I sat next to PFC McMahon. He showed me the scars from jungle rot. Didn't want to talk about much of anything. I remember that we were so grateful for cold milk on the flight, Dwayne said.

September 17, 1971

Dwayne and I went to the NCO club to eat crab claws, smoke and drink beer. The night before, I had been assigned to guard duty at the Officer's Club. The club closed at 1:00 AM. Tables around the pool were littered with overflowing ashtrays, some empty and some half-empty beer bottles, wine and cocktail glasses. I smashed several with my guard-duty baton.

I was starting to inhale Dwayne's bitterness along with the haze in the NCO club.

Sitting across from me in the booth with his feet propped on the bench I sat on, he told me part of his story. How can I make it real? As I write, I fear I will fictionalize and distort with words Dwayne's damaged heart, mind and soul.

Dwayne spoke of his naivete when he arrived in Vietnam. He was nineteen and combat eager—ready to try his new skills and anxious to get out of the combat center—its inc-country orientation sessions and into the field.

He was called a "newfer" and looked at it. Combat-ready in his new gear, clean-shaven face and shining faith in Uncle Sam's army, he watched the scenery slipping past beneath the open door of the chopper. Lush green foliage and a mirage of harmony and peace hid the horror beneath. Night slammed into him. He was dumped like a COD package amid the firebase dust. It wasn't what he expected, but those about to be coptered out fully expected him. He didn't know at the time that they were headed for Flying Tiger airlines for a ride back to the world.

Sometime in October 1971

These are my words as I recall late-night talks with Dwayne. A tape recorder would have made it much easier to put this in Dwayne's words.

He told me about his first patrol moving off the firebase. They approached a rice paddy after humping for an hour. The day before, four guys had been caught in an ambush. He said he felt fear and death become real. He saw himself lying face down in the rice paddy muck. He was lucky that day, but nameless days and nights lay ahead.

He spent the next month wading, sloshing, sometimes walking point, body caking with mud, shivering, sweating, crawling, cowering, crying silently while nerves screamed. More patrols, guard duty, huddling against the rain, walking nerves to sleep, vomiting, losing faith, dying every time he saw a filled body bag.

Dwayne said that reflexes came quicker than thought. Instinct sent his body crushing into the ground, trying to crawl deeper as the first sounds of bursts of bullets. Cover meant life and the ability to fight back, to stay alive, and to keep others alive. Life was reduced to torn flesh, the stench of death, the knowing death came this way.

He Told Me

There had been too many second lieutenants' mistakes that sent boys home in body bags. Too many nights of raw nerves and exhaustive explosions. Too many times, he'd felt the loss of sanity even under seemingly normal times. He was fourteen months out of combat and thirty months into military madness.

In the here and now of barracks living and officc duty, he said he could hear the bawling apologies and pleading of an ROTC captain for troops to stand down after VC snipers put a hole in Billy Bates' forehead. Dwayne resisted the urge to shoot the captain. He needed someone to attack even now, maybe for the rest of his life. He needed a switch to flip to turn off his rage. Who would listen? He squeezed his fist.

My note: I still see Dwayne's ready-to-explode face. That face was spreading everywhere in America by thousands of Dwayne's-of-Vietnam. I cannot tell his story to eyes and hearts that turn away. Displaced veterans like Dwayne will succumb to the poverty of their souls and they will die in the alleys of our free nation.

Later (I didn't want to hear more)

Either he or I was becoming delusional. I knew nothing except what Dwayne told me.

Hours were infused with boozy stories. I listened and made notes.

Supply drops from choppers became circuses of sharing. Morale was boosted as they bartered to trade rations. There was love in surviving together. Dying became nothingness—a vacuum like the wind rushing out. God had nothing to do with it. A bullet. Tripwire. RPG.

NOTES:

***Pastiche**

-Firebase night attack

-Body bag a buddy

-Colonel's remarks about identifying bodies

-Malaria, recuperation

-Decisions to re-up

-Chaplain's remarks

-Night ambush

-Setting up trip flares

-Attempted mutiny

-Hooch maids

-Donut dollies

-Hot soda

-Hot beer

*Pastiche: dramatic literary or musical piece openly imitating a previous work—often with satirical intent gone lazy.

After Note:

Thanksgiving 1973

Dwayne re-upped. I moved to Chicago. Needed to leave the army and Eyota behind.

I haven't heard from Dwayne in months. Wonder why? I suspect he will not get in touch until he mails the promised package. Maybe he was caught for using the post telephone for private use. Maybe he's been busted for taking extra weeks of leave without permission or telling anyone. Maybe he's in jail for stealing Blaze Stars' dressing room toilet seat. I wrote him to COD it to me.

Asking a Fisherman About Hate

Our flashlights sever
        indecently exposed worms as
    they slurp across the lawn.
My thumb and forefinger don't belong there
Clothes pinned to their nakedness.

I speak to your laughter,
    telling you to read poems.
        You say you despise poetry.

I ask how a fisherman hates:
        Is it the night crawler's fate?
        Its drowning on death-bent hooks?

If the lake were my earth for tunneling,
I'd question the moonlight's depth by
        counting pain in spiraled
        grass stains on my elbow.

If the earth were your lake for fishing,

You'd sample the minnow tanks by
    baptizing palms in swirling
    mud puddles in your yard.

Perhaps we'll recognize our sameness while
We sit on the deck peeling mud from
    Scabs of our day-without-fish
    you telling of filleting bursts of sun
    I of seeing the poet bleeding in the sink.

Falling

A sun shower foams
spills rainbow trout.
My eyes are hooked
to their underbellies,
My hand snags
on weeds
whose earth-clutching roots
snag this fisher's dreams.

The Ice House

I hear the wind piling drifts on the steps.

Inside this house, my lamp throbs; welcome to the fisher
Whose barbed fingers cast a line at the frosted window.

I crawl beneath patches in a hand-stitched quilt.

My father's father lies beside me, a fleshy frame
Wrapped in monofilament fishing line.

His needled breath punctures my pain.

And we float together like fishbones
Swirling down a hole in a frozen lake.

An Unnoticed Drowning

When we paused our fishing,
I watched you glance at my reflection
Before shattering it with a hook and sinker.

We fish from a bottomless boat
Laden with peopled rocks
Buoyed by lifejackets.

We row in circles
Careful not to spill
A speck of ourselves.

We littered the shore
With our weekend cottage
Pebbled the beach with children.

After we dock,
Will anyone notice
Should they drag the lake for us?

A Child's Guide to Identification

A disjointed caterwauling

Breaks through slate-gray folds

Of my bedroom curtains.

I had fed eggs to a hobo

Scrambled them myself while

Mom was Sunday churching

Dad was Walleye piking.

I listen for a rose-colored cat to purr quietly.

Blood

I did not cause the blood

to run

from my son's mouth.

Yet it is mine.

He has bitten into my past.

I wince at the smile

between his learning tears,

blue fins

swimming in his eyes

peel the cataracts

of my backward vision.

Silencers

I skip pebbles

On the lake

Hoping to silence

The echo of a loon.

White boats draw blood

From the sun

Their rusted oarlocks click

And I feel once more

The loss of my son.

Business is Good

I think of the N.R.A. Certificate of Achievement
I have won.
I think of the Vietnam Service Medal
That is mine.

Sumac branches snap
As I stumble search for grouse
But my 12 gauge will protect me
From falling into the earth
That is mine.

The natural order reminds me
Business is good.
But eyes ride upon my back.
Eyes wait in ambush to repair footsteps.
That also are mine.

Severings

He came today

 the owner of newborn calves

To fix barbed strands

 severed in clovered grass

To spade-scrape glass,

 cracked chrome, gasoline soak

In earth dark safety.

"I will not help.

 Nor will I mourn.

I've chipmunks. Squirrels.

Wrens. Jays. Who feed

 without fear.

"They die," I said

Nodding with the wind surge.

 Bending to his task.

Eyes hand shaded.

 He looked to the sun.

Glass buried. Fence repaired.

 Spade in hand.

He looked at me.

"Done," he said

Boots

Cold crunches beneath my cat's paw boot,
        presses the earth
            seeking warmth in powdered footprints.
Snow bare weeds quiver blue against the snow,
            silencing my summer cry for warm shadows.
My mind wanders over all I have passed,
            through bent-weed footsteps,
                    to crushed cattail muskrat huts
Where I would not pause for warmth.

No One Shoots Songbirds

No one shoots songbirds anymore
Not even Chief Red Cloud
Who bangs his wagon against
My car's virgin fender.
It's strange to watch robins
Pull at the earth while a child's
War whoops splinter my window screen.

I played once, pretending grandpa's farm,
Was African Jungle. Striped barn cats
Were my tiger prey.

I played once until I grew into hunting boots
With rawhide laces and silver eyelets.
Oh, how I grew. Out of myself into manhood
Straight out of Outdoor Life and Sear's Catalog.

I learned to use my peep sights
To keep my observations silent.
I learned to stalk grouse

To still shiver on my spine.

I learned to cradle my 12-gauge shotgun

To protect its barrel from bramble scratches.

But now I walk alone

With silence

Disturbing

My hunt.

November 11, 1974

I feel eyes riding upon my back
  While I sever sumac branches
  Stumble-searching for white-tailed deer.
I can ignore the weight if I think
  of N.R.A. Bulls Eye Trophies I have won
or
  of the Vietnam Service Medal that is mine.
After all, the war is over. I am home.
  My rifle will protect me
  From falling into the earth
  Too soon.
Flakes of snow chill my cheek
  Fall to soften crisp leaves
  That moment before had staccato my steps,
I can stalk silently if I think
  of each branch containing a trip-wired grenade
or
  of the Purple Heart that is mine.
I see a deer. A Trophy buck.
  His eyes tell me
  my war is over.

Sunset

An old woman walks the dark streets

Tears of goodbye sunsets

Spot her shopping bag

Snow slicks the curb

For her stepping

Down

Public Speaking

My body conspires against me,
brain screaming at heart
to rush blood to the face
splashing it on cheeks
to drip like a newly painted barn.
Simultaneously, the malfunctioning message center
pulses, "Your fly is open. Your fly is open.
Your fly is open." Again, and again, and again.
I'll check. But how? How do I slyly
slide a finger the infinite distance
from public exposure to private security?
Ignore it. Ignore it. Ignore it.
No way. No way. No way.
I've got it. Continue talking, raising the voice
to focus attention more clearly
on the face and voice.
Loudly now. That's it.
Now, slowly slide your thumb behind the belt buckle,
tucking in that bulging shred of the shirt.
Simultaneously, flick the little finger,

checking and praying the zipper

is at the top.

Two Trees in April

I have a Christmas tree on my porch

not quite picked clean

of its cranberry garlands

wrapping its limbs

with frayed-bow bandages.

Becomes a Good Friday tree

spruced up for a resurrection day.

Its needles

poised

to puncture the sunset.

Hanging

Oak logs glow like groin fire.
  Thunder in the blizzard
    simmering into occasional explosions,
    oak-white foam, red heat
    crumbling into dust on the hearth
    like a hardening fog.
Squirrels hang from tree branches,
    scoop cracked corn from the bird feeder.
    This country place is fire
    and lights dimming in my mind.
    I've sat down here to meet myself.
A car swishes through the silence
    of my mind like a sparrow
    flopping about in the chimney.
    My rafters collect cobweb kites
    as I stare at the ceiling
    because I've lost the string.

The Crossing

I watch moonlight bake snow loaves

in tombstone pans.

A skier has crossed the crust

hurriedly

as if he were weaving a shutter

to cover corpses.

But the window from which I watch

is open,

reflecting the eyes of a stillborn child.

I say no rosaries here.

For all of this, I speak to snow-eagled angels

as if they would rise

to lift this icy vision

beyond the hill

where there are no stones.

Unchildish Rain

A cloud is cored
like a watermelon.
Ice sprinkles through,
salts upturned lilac lips
that quiver when the wind
bends down to pick them.
Water fills the vase with petals
Petals that might have scented
the dew on a calmer day.

Following Walk's Wind

Cold crouches beneath my cat's paw boot
Slinks, smoke-breathed
Into frozen footprint
To avoid shadowed arrows
Launched from snow-bare weeds
Quivering blue in later-winter light.

My mind wanders over all I have passed
Through bent-weed footsteps
To crushed cattail muskrat huts
Where I clawed at iced mud stalks
Seeking to clutch warmth inside the den.

Fall Hunting

Wood Clinched

I feel best
In red-black flannel
Flecked with wood dust
Sharp from the sun,
When my eyebrow sweat
Quivers from sun squints.

But my thoughts
Grind bloody
Because I remember
Silent screams
Whirled in wakes
Where I stepped
Carelessly
Scattering
Ducks.

Wine Makings

I swim through the August heat
Swatting gnatted chunks of air
With a free-hand paddle.

Sandburs cling to shoelaces
Like first knots tied by a child.
Dust paints my face a clown mask.

Sound of my plastic bucket's thud
Against my thigh keeps my pace
Synchronized with the earth.

I sip wine from imaginary bottles
Step carefully over bloody glass
Strewn over crushed chokecherries.

Chokecherries ripe and smashed
By marksmen's bullets, boots
Broken soda bottles.

I scoop fragmented fruit

Ripping my finger

For a taste of blood and wine.

Bow Hunter

My brother slung his rope
Over the snow-furred tree
Pulled and pulled
Until his neck muscles
Bulged like the damp eyes
Of the doe, he hung.

Forcing the doe's belly-slit
Apart from the forked-stick wedge
He knotted his lips
To tie down his pulse
Withdrew finger-strings
Nocked with spoiled blood.

A Song for Deer

Come down with me
Into the bore of the rifle
Into the circle of the rope
Come down with me

Soon there will be explosions of light
Daystar bursting through clouds
Spirits fill the air with smell of dust
Leaves weaving lattice lairs in the air.

Come down with me
Into the gash of the wound
Into the stomach of the pill
Come down with me

Sunday, there will be organ grindings

Epilogue

A Prose Poem
Inspired by Morrison's Sulu

In the moments awakening from sleep, what is it I am supposed to feel?

And where is my body and why do words confuse me?

For the next few seconds, I'm going to crawl back inside the envelope

Of time between sleep and awake. Come with me.

There is space here for one or two, or two hundred million of us.

Each of us can taste the remains of last night's lipstick on our lips.

We marvel at the ripe apple smell as it soothes our lungs.

The two of us smother the gray breaths of millions who dissolve in the mists.

Reaching through space with arms outstretched toward the light of the waking day

I rope off a corner when we can stay for just a second longer.

But you are gone. Swallowed by our clothes and your obligations.

Will you be late? Is our laundry done?

My legs lift me toward the light. My shoulders pin me to the shadows.

Pain shatters the prism of clearing head.

I hear the breaking of glass

Am startled to see my face shatter in the mirror.

For Sisters Five

White fleece

Your face

Beneath quilted dreams

Your eyes

Wavering wind

Your hands

Snow

Rise

Rise

Wrap your body

In my skin

So you

Glow again

After Words

I thought, digging for words
To give as a gift
Would be easy spadework
But much of the ground sprouts rocks.

I would not struggle to raise blisters
If there were another way.
Leaning on shovel's handle
I stare at shadowed words
Resting in the earth.

A burst of sunlight
Tells me to feel the sky,
To wrap around my shoulders
So I'll never be cold.

Whatever I touch
Crack its cocoon gently
Lest I break the wing of a butterfly.

Seek truth from words, so they do not lie

Fallow among the rocks.

Not Much to It

There really isn't much to it.
No shock there at all.
But rather like leaves
Burning gold from frost,
Or birch logs consuming.

There really isn't much to it.
No shock there at all.
Smiles of children laughing
Well-worn books upon the hearth.

"What?" you ask.
"Oh. I don't know.
Maybe if you like
We'll call it remembering
Loving, living
Or dying
Perhaps.

Acknowledgements

Special thanks to:

- Mark Chirhart for Poetry Review.
- Kris Fix for Poetry Clerical Work.
- Mark Kalla for Prose Review.
- Robert Pennington for Prose Review.
- Richard Hammel posthumously for his enduring friendship John Cartwright www.artrail.com (Artrail—John Cartwright—Artist of Upper Midwest Railroading—Home page) for permission to use his drawing for the cover.

Printed in the USA
CPSIA information can be obtained
at www.ICGtesting.com
LVHW022148051023
760329LV00034B/1009

9 781088 094457